IMAGES OF ENGLAND

NEWCASTLE-UNDER-LYME REVISITED

IMAGES OF ENGLAND

NEWCASTLE–
UNDER–LYME
REVISITED

NEIL COLLINGWOOD AND
GREGOR SHUFFLEBOTHAM

The
History
Press

This book is dedicated to the late William Colville who, although a native of Leith, Edinburgh lived for many years in the borough and left a valuable legacy to Newcastle people by photographing things that no one else did.

Frontispiece: A view from Queen's Gardens towards Nelson Place by E. Harrison & Son, *c*. 1935. The gardens were created from the former grounds of St Giles Rectory, now Rectory Chambers, built in 1698.

First published in 2005 by Tempus Publishing

Reprinted in 2009 by
The History Press
The Mill, Brimscombe Port,
Stroud, Gloucestershire, GL5 2QG
www.thehistorypress.co.uk

Reprinted 2013

British Library Cataloguing in Publication Data.
A catalogue record for this book is available from the British Library.

ISBN 978 0 7524 3672 2

Typesetting and origination by
Tempus Publishing Limited.
Printed in Great Britain.

Contents

Acknowledgements

Betley Local History Society 21A, 41B, 68B; Sheila Bonehill 30A, 30B; John S. Booth 60A, 60B, 86B; Mike Brown 105B, 127B; Bradwell Methodist Church 26A, 26B, 28B, 31B, 32B, 114B; Roy Burden 78B; Beryl Carter 55B, 71B; N. Collingwood 52A/B, 99A, 110B, 113A, 114A, 115B; William Colville (The Colville Collection) 46B, 47B, 48A, 48B, 49A, 49B, 50B, 73A, 74B, 75A, 75B, 82B, 94B, 102A, 102B, 103A, 103B, 104A, 104B, 105A, 118A, 118B, 119A, 119B, 120A, 120B; Rex & C. Downing: 16A, 24A, 24B, 28A, 43A; Meg Durber 19B, 20A, 23A, 23B, 63A, 99B; P.B. Dyson 96A, 96B, 97A; Joe Ewing/Clayton Lodge Hotel 56A; The Family and descendants of E.S. Grogan 58A; Sheila Grove 100A, 109B; Hopkinson, Wootton & Lovatt 12/13; Spencer Jackson 21B; Audrey Lawton 36B, 62A, 62B, 63B; E.R. Morten 121A; Anne Mulliner 18A, 18B, 19A, 29B, 113B; Newcastle-under-Lyme School 44B, 65B, 80A; C. & J. Shone 43B, 44A, 110A; S. Shufflebotham 34B; E. & J. Wade 11A, 11B, 14A, 14B, 15A; Susan Williamson 41A, 50A 124A, 124B, 125A, 125B, 126B, 127A. The remaining images are from the Shufflebotham Collection.

We would also like to offer our thanks to the following for their assistance in completing this book: Allan C. Baker, John Bishop, Wendy Butler, Delyth Copp, Neil Dobbin, Sue Fox, Jim Goddard, Newcastle-under-Lyme Reference Library, Edward Paice, Staffordshire Regiment Museum, Allen Tipton, Keith Twigg, Jeremy Crick, Helen Waller, Louise Taylor.

The bandstand in Stubbs Walks (*c.* 1930) by William Parton. Stubbs Walks was part of the Town Walks, opened in 1816 as part of the agreement for 'inclosure' of the common fields. Newcastle's 'upper canal' originally terminated here.

Introduction

Newcastle-under-Lyme has been in existence since the middle of the twelfth century and the commonly held belief is that the town developed in the same way that a *vicus* would have developed outside a Roman garrison a thousand years earlier. A *vicus* was a settlement for traders who supplied goods and services such as food, clothing, weaponry and a range of entertainments for off-duty hours to the inhabitants of the fort. Within the present Borough of Newcastle the Roman fort at Chesterton had such a settlement and Newcastle town itself is believed to have had similar origins. Newcastle's medieval castle, of which virtually nothing remains above ground today, was built on the strategic road junction where the road to Nantwich and Chester branched off the main London to Carlisle route. Initially a humble village stood near the castle and this grew into a small market town, before enjoying a meteoric rise in prosperity and importance later. This rise in status was generated by the granting of a Royal Charter by Henry II in 1173, coupled with the town's position at the hub of the area's road network. The charter liberated the newly elevated 'freemen' to develop the town's commerce, providing Newcastle's Lord of the Manor, the King, with a steadily increasing income from taxes levied on the burgesses' business dealings.

Throughout subsequent centuries Newcastle continued to develop and prosper until, by the eighteenth century, the population included the majority of the area's doctors, lawyers and bankers and the town had become in effect the capital of North Staffordshire. Elegant Georgian houses were built, many of which still survive today, and the traders exploited the convenient road connections to the full. Coaching inns in the town were large and numerous and many businesses plied their trade transporting people, goods and mail between places such as London and Manchester. Over the same period one particular trade, the making of felt hats, had developed to the point where it employed the majority of the town's working population. For about three centuries the trade flourished, with large numbers of hats being sent not only to London but also overseas to America. Then, just before the middle of the nineteenth century, the trade collapsed and the factories closed. Skilled hatters were forced either to learn new trades or else move to places where the hatting trade was not yet in decline. The hat factories had disappeared by the time the first cameras were being set up and although one or two former textile mills still linger on in the town, no trace of even the largest of the hat factories survives. Even the fine Georgian house on London Road formerly occupied by William Mason, the owner of a hat factory which employed several hundred people, has recently been demolished. Despite this sad loss, many buildings which existed when Newcastle still made hats are pictured within this book, together with a record of various other trades followed by Newcastle's people. These include the mining of coal, clay, ironstone and other minerals and the manufacture of bricks, tiles, paper, iron and steel, together with many service industries.

The images for this second Tempus Images of England volume on Newcastle-under-Lyme have been obtained from people who in many cases had no idea that the photographs stored in their biscuit tins or old suitcases were of any interest to anyone. This has proved to be far from the truth, as trawling through any cache of old family photographs usually reveals at least one image that, if not actually important as a historical record, is at least interesting for some reason. An old black and white photograph of a family member in front of his/her place of work may just turn out to be the only photograph in existence of that factory, shop, hotel or hole in the ground.

A view along The Avenue, Basford, *c.* 1905. This was formerly the drive to Basford Hall and the photograph was taken from close to the lodge, demolished in around 1980.

The compilers of this work have between them lived in the Borough of Newcastle for nearly 110 years and have witnessed the way in which the pace of change has accelerated markedly since the early 1960s. Both remember many buildings which no longer stand in the positions they occupied for centuries and vistas that have been lost forever. They remember days when few people had cars and when collecting 'car numbers' was an enjoyable children's pastime; when rag and bone men exchanged scrap for goldfish in plastic bags off the back of their carts and the clip-clop of hooves on the road signalled the arrival of the coal-man. Not so long ago it was possible to catch a train to Hanley and see the eastern sky aglow with the flames of Shelton Bar's blast furnaces. In the same way that such memories are now history, today's young children will be astonished to learn that there was once a North Staffordshire Coalfield and that every day local men would risk their lives to travel a vertical mile underground to work. There will always be a place for photographs of the local area and it is hoped a hardcore of picture-takers will continue to record the changing landscape on negatives, just as Edwin Harrison did nearly a century and a half ago.

The authors hope that within this selection of images there will be something to interest everyone living in our 'Loyal and Ancient Borough'. With increased leisure-time, people's interests have become wide and varied and such subjects as Joe Edwards' motorcycle on page 21, the tarmac works on pages 18 and 19 and Wootton's Hearse on pages 12 and 13 have already generated much interest. The vast majority of the pictures have not been published before and because of the way they have been stored their quality varies. Where images of inferior quality have been used, this is likely to be because they are very unusual, perhaps even unique, and therefore worthy of being shown. The compilers hope that readers will appreciate and enjoy their selection of images and the snapshots of the past that they represent.

Neil Collingwood and Gregor Shufflebotham
24 May 2005

one

Horses to Horse-Power

GROWN WITH
HADFIELD'S
SPECIAL MANGOLD
MANURE.

This card shows how heavy horses were used before tractors became the universal farm tool. This picture was taken at Domvilles Farm near Audley, located close to the M6 at the western edge of the borough. The Challinors moved here in around 1884 when Daniel Booth, the then owner, went bankrupt. In 1886 T. Challinor advertised in the *Staffordshire Advertiser* for a wagoner, perhaps the man shown holding the bridle above.

Although it is not known where this photograph was taken or who the subjects were, the photographer was William Parton, who was active in Newcastle between 1896 and around 1950, although the style of dress here suggests a date of around 1900. It is easy to imagine this being the family of a vicar from a rural parish such as Betley or Madeley, posing in their sporty new gig.

While horses were important both for riding and hauling vehicles, many businesses prospered supplying equestrian equipment. Here J.T. Burke (left) and his son Albert pose outside their Higherland saddlery, next door to the Wagon & Horses. The business was established around 1900, selling and repairing saddles, harnesses and collars for draught horses. 'Old Joe' the dog steadfastly refused to look at the camera.

Burke & Sons were successful because they were not left behind by progress. As the number of motor vehicles increased, the Burkes enlarged their shop, converting their saddlery to a 'Motor Spirit & Oil Depot'; here William Edward Burke stands proudly next to the pumps. An advertisement for Mobil Oil dates this photograph to 1920 or later. Other familiar names visible in the photograph are Castrol, Michelin, Shell and Dunlop.

This hearse belonged to Wolstanton undertakers Woottons, still trading today as Hopkinson, Wootton & Lovatt. The man in black is believed to be Cornelius Wootton and the driver his son Cornelius Junior. The hearse stands on the present site of the war memorial outside St Margaret's Church and the

photographer was Frederick Hall, who operated from High Street in Wolstanton between 1907 and 1912, dating the picture quite precisely.

The first 'Higherland Garage' was built in the 1930s on the site where the modern service station stands today. During the Second World War the hangar-like building housed an aircraft which was used for training Fleet Air Arm mechanics from HMS *Daedalus*, as Clayton Hall was known during the war. This picture probably dates from around the early 1960s, the garage finally being demolished in 1965.

This is Burke's filling station following the demolition of the saddlery. It remained like this well into the 1960s, when a drive-in establishment was built over the site of the first Higherland Garage. Not only were petrol and car accessories for sale here, but also bicycle spares and repairs. The building just visible above the roof is the Wagon & Horses.

The second Higherland Garage pictured in the mid-1960s, when a Ford Cortina Mk 1 was too expensive for most Newcastle motorists and a used 1950s Consul, Zephyr or Zodiac had to suffice. As the sign shows, this garage, built in 1953, was located on the corner of Deansgate and Seabridge Road, opposite the Sneyd Arms. Extensively modernised and with a new upper floor, this building still stands today.

A 1914 Potteries Electric Traction Co. Ltd Daimler CD bus stands outside Sutherland House, now the entrance to the Roebuck Centre. During the First World War most of the fleet was requisitioned to France, forcing PET to buy second-hand buses to maintain services. This example was purchased from Sheerness Tramways in around 1916. It had had its charabanc body replaced in around 1920 and pneumatic tyres were fitted soon after this picture was taken.

Left: The menfolk of the Downing family of Springfield, Bradwell with their 1927 Austin Windsor 12/4 Heavy. From left to right are Henshall Guy, Charles Ernest, Clive James and possibly George Hodgkinson Downing. Springfield was a large house located almost opposite Bradwell Hospital, demolished when the road became a dual carriageway. In the background is Farcroft, later to become the Fanny Deakin Maternity Hospital.

Below: This 1930s view of Red Lion Square, possibly taken from upstairs at Clement Wain's, gives an impression of Newcastle after the ages of the horse and the tram had come to an end. Horse-drawn carts would continue to be used by coal merchants and rag and bone men for some years but the dominance of the motor vehicle was now evident; horses had indeed given way to horse-power.

two

Work...

Apedale Slag and Tarmacadam Works in the 1920s. This mound is the Victorian slag-tip formed from slag produced in the cold blast process. This was better for making tarmac than later hot blast slag. The slag was crushed and graded before being mixed with tar to produce tarmacadam. The men would load the material into the narrow-gauge trucks, which were probably then pushed by hand to the plant (see following pictures) ready for processing.

The slag mound on the right is the same as that seen in the previous picture and one of the structures on the left can be seen in the following photograph. Tarmacadam's advantage over plain macadam road surfaces was that it was more stable and less dusty in dry weather. Apedale ironworks, which were closed and demolished in 1930, are visible behind the tarmac plant on the left, dating the pictures to the 1920s.

These men's clothes clearly indicate their status at the tarmac plant. The two on the left at the rear, one of whom is probably Mr Grice, sport ties and are clearly managers, whereas the other three are manual workers, possibly foremen. The wife of George Simpson (the man at front right) used to complain that she was always having to repair his torn moleskin trousers.

Helen Boardman (aged five) and Josephine Weeks (aged three) sitting on Burley Bridge over the Gresley Canal in 1946. The canal was completed in 1778 to facilitate the transport of coal and other materials from Apedale to Newcastle. From there it could be transported via the 'lower canal' to the Potteries. Behind the girls can be seen Chesterton Tile Works, which had more than thirty beehive ovens when it was taken over by G.H. Downing in 1938.

Bunkers Hill Pit in Talke, which possessed one of the very few tandem headgears used in the North Staffordshire coalfield. The colliery opened in around 1850 and twenty-five years later, in April 1875, a firedamp explosion probably caused by shot-firing claimed the lives of forty-three miners. Difficult though it is to believe, in the 1890s this pit employed 290 men underground and a further ninety on the surface.

Silverdale Colliery, c. 1980. In the centre are the bath and lamphouses and in the background are Drifts ('dips') 1, 2 and 3, which descended 4,000m at a gradient of 1:4. At the pit bottom, 1,000m down, galleries radiated outwards and sometimes further downwards following the coal seams. British Coal ceased mining in 1993, but under various ownerships Silverdale continued in production until 1998, becoming the last North Staffordshire pit working.

Joe Edwards pictured here in Middle Street in Leycett, *c.* 1950. Joe worked as a miner for over fifty years and bought his 1949 James Cadet Deluxe motorcycle to save himself having to catch the bus between his home in Betley and Leycett Colliery. The motorcycle appears to be fairly new and has a number of optional extras fitted. In earlier times miners from Betley walked to Leycett, a distance of about three miles.

Charlie and Reg Jackson in around 1925 with their new lorry. The family business previously employed a cart but one night Charlie said, 'Mother, we'll have to have one of those newfangled lorries soon. Those men with lorries are shifting more coal than we are, and doing more trips a day.' The lorry, bought from Pepper's Garage the following day, transported coal from Parkhouse Colliery to nearby Metallic Tileries, but regular punctures necessitated the fitting of solid rear tyres.

The Stantons' work involved travelling in their caravan giving performances wherever they could obtain bookings; the tiny pony possibly suggests a comic element to their act. They described themselves as 'Royal Entertainers', but it is unknown how they justified this claim. Perhaps the Stantons performed at one of Ewart Grogan's Camp Hill parties.

There was pressure on beds here at Newcastle Isolation Hospital, next to the cemetery, during an epidemic of lupins. Working there appears to have allowed for a reasonable degree of freedom, as photographs exist of nurses sitting in the gardens often accompanied by a dog, petting a pony or, as here, admiring the plants. The nature of infectious diseases perhaps made the hospital manic at times and virtually empty at others.

Above: Looking every bit the film star, the twenty-eight-year-old Princess Margaret poses with the directors of Rists Wires & Cables Ltd during a royal visit on 9 December 1958. Her sister Princess Elizabeth had paid a similar visit to Enderley Mills on 2 November 1949. Four years older than Margaret, Elizabeth was always seen as the serious and dutiful sister, while Margaret lived life to the full.

Right: Friends and workmates Meg Rhodes, Louis Johnson, Brenda Pointon and Elsie Timmis pose outside Matthews' shop during a break from their work as machinists at Enderley Mills. Built in 1881, the mill remained open until the 1990s. After it burned down it was discovered that the mill was standing on a huge Victorian bottle dump, although sadly most of the material was removed by unauthorised collectors before it could be properly recorded.

Left: A young Henshall Downing poses with a worker at the family tileworks. The man, wearing gloves to protect his hands from cuts, leans a number of roof tiles against a solid upright and uses a narrow hammer to chip imperfections from their edges. G.H. (Harry) Downing, Henshall's uncle, headed what became the largest roof tile manufacturing company in the world.

Below: Probably taken on the occasion of the retirement of the matron, Mrs E. Gooding, this photograph shows the staff at Newcastle Isolation Hospital in 1949. To the right of the matron is Sister Beryl Downing, the next matron, and on the other side is Sister Williams. On the back row are the two hospital gardeners/handymen, on the left Sam Wagstaffe and on the right Jack Williamson. The Isolation Hospital in Cemetery Road later became a geriatric hospital and was renamed 'Lymewood Hospital'.

three

...and Play

This June 1958 photograph shows a dilemma faced by teenagers for half a century. These four Teddy boys are attending Bradwell church dressed with varying degrees of defiance, with John Thorneycroft pointedly refusing to face the speaker. His entourage, including Dennis Humphries and Arthur Bebbington, assume indifference, yet listen attentively. Rebellious John recently retired as senior design engineer at Michelin and now organises a bowls club.

A comparison of this picture with the previous image shows another side of youth culture in the church. This unknown skiffle group, photographed at Bradwell, is almost certainly playing songs with a Christian motif, but in a contemporary style. Their clothes and haircuts are fashionable, yet giving it his all on the tea chest bass is their minister, complete with dog collar.

Above: A rare 1913 picture of the Wolstanton Amateurs Cricket Club team at a time when they would have been somewhat overshadowed, or possibly inspired, by their near neighbours Porthill Park CC. Porthill topped the North Staffordshire & District League convincingly that season, losing only once in twenty-two matches.

Right: A major reason for Porthill Park's dominance of local cricket prior to the First World War was the presence in their team from 1906 to 1914 of the legendary Staffordshire and England bowler Sydney Francis Barnes, seen here in 1913. During this period Barnes took 893 wickets for the club at an average of only 5.29 runs per wicket, helping Porthill to top the North Staffs & District League six times.

This Christmas scene was photographed at Newcastle Isolation Hospital in the 1940s. On the left is the matron, Mrs E. Gooding, formerly assistant matron at Bradwell Hospital. The distinct lack of children in this ward scene was perhaps because most of them were hiding from the terrifying individual in the back row. And who was that standing *next* to the mayor?

A fancy dress parade at Bradwell Methodist Church, *c.* 1960. Annie Oakley (third from left in the front row) seems to be undergoing something of a calamity – her awkward stance and ill-timed blink make her look as though she has been partaking too freely of the sipping whiskey!

Ashfields Wesleyan Methodist Church football team pose for the 1906/07 season team photograph outside a corrugated-iron shed presumably used as a changing room. William Harold Brown, later to become a founding partner in Queen Street solicitors Brown & Corbishley and also Deputy Town Clerk of Newcastle, is sitting in the front row, to the right of the captain.

Spot the ball on a misty day in the 1950s at Roe Lane Sports Field, Westlands, with generously tailored shorts much in evidence. Spectators cluster by the pavilion, with its catering facilities and changing rooms, while on the right Ken Mulliner, playing for BTH, waits for a cross. Although the Westlands was expanding south towards Clayton, the playing fields, near Roe Lane Farm, were still surrounded by countryside.

Above: Bradwell Methodist Youth Club activities tableau in 1953, including Joan Ashley, Dorothy Salt, Marilyn Currie, Alan Davenport, Graham Booth, John Glover, Muriel Scott, Mavis Bucknall, Bert Baddeley, Beryl and Winnie Dunn, Molly Maland, 'Queen' Jean Shone and her brother Clive, Jean Hancock and Maureen Beech. Each year at the youth club anniversary festival the previous year's photograph would be used to allow youth club members to be posed for that year's picture.

Left: Cheshire Joint Sanatorium's July 1957 *Germ Magazine,* hot off the press. The magazine was published internally twice a year and patients submitted articles, poems, stories or observations on life inside for publication. Sheila Bennett (third from left) of Croft Street spent nine months at the Loggerheads Sanatorium following a mass X-ray, despite never actually being ill. Sheila was fortunate as some patients required stays of two years.

Opposite below: Bradwell Methodist Church and Youth Centre football team for the 1952/53 season pose by the youth club, with youth leader Mr W.A. Cockell standing to the left of the goalkeeper. Team captain Stan Walker sits front centre of the team and its supporters, who include Jimmy Jones, Reg Cross, Stan Wragg, Ron Weaver, Les Wilkes, John Glover and Fred Garside.

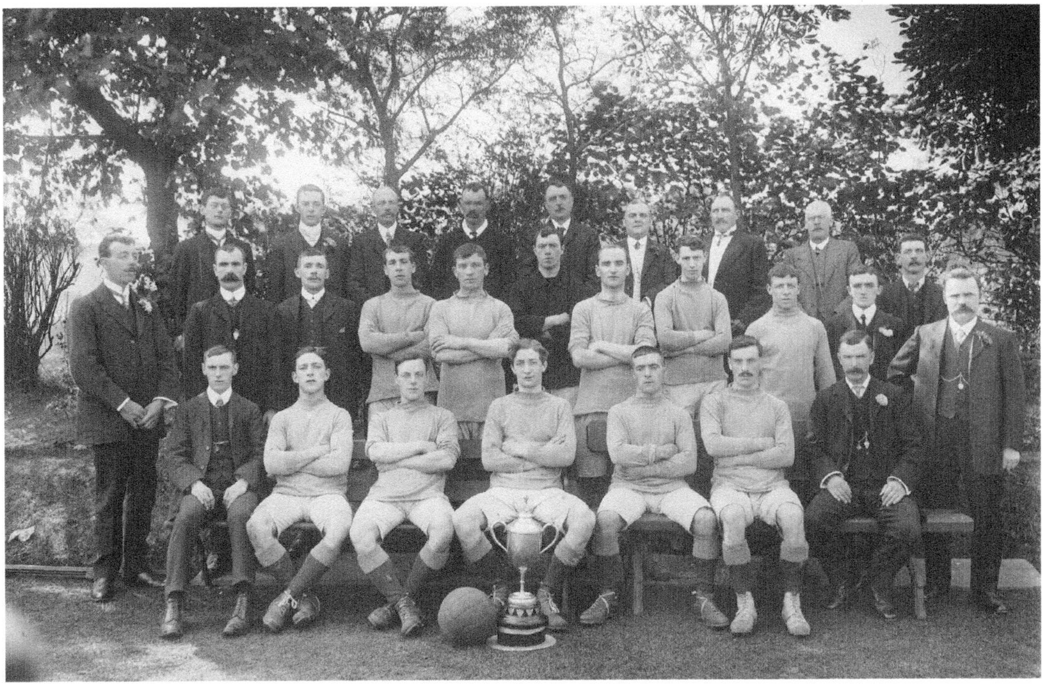

Above: The Newcastle Town FC team and officials proudly display the May Bank Cup, having beaten Goldenhill Wanderers 2-0 at Cobridge in the final on 24 April 1911. The team are, from left to right, front row: W. Spooner, R. Smith, J. Grady, F. Casewell, C. Smith. Middle row: A. Pointon, J. Tryner, H. Ward, H. Wolfe (captain), E. Cook, A. Jervis. The officials include chairman Mr G. Smith, vice-president Mr W. Meadon and treasurer Mr W. Machin.

This 1920s carnival queen was photographed in Heathcote Road, Miles Green. The card is one of a set of at least four which show a carnival procession en route through the villages which surround Audley, and it seems likely that the young lady was probably the Audley carnival queen. Carnivals were popular in Audley and many of them were recorded by local photographer Thomas Warham.

It is difficult to imagine a group of today's teenage girls being prepared to subject themselves to this the annual crowning of the Bradwell Youth Club festival queen. On the right is the new queen and her retinue and to the left the outgoing queen, Jennifer Capewell, with hers. Also in the group is Joan Whitehall and, on the extreme left, Sylvia Banks. Can you name any of the others?

This school cricket team of enthusiastic-looking young local players in the 1920s may lack the right kit and have what seems to be very well-used equipment, but they appear no less eager to compete. They are pictured here by local photographer Henry D. Taylor of Vessey Terrace.

Undoubtedly one of many similar events around the country on 2 June 1953, the Thistleberry Avenue area Coronation party is in full swing at the Unitarian Meeting House by St Giles' Church. Owing to a lack of available public transport, parents and children were driven there in a convoy of private cars. Among the children enjoying themselves are Billy Barnes, Sheila Trickett, Philip Elkes, Martin Hall and David Parker.

Left: These interestingly dressed ladies were photographed on the top of their workplace, the Co-operative Society Emporium in Ironmarket. The Co-op regularly organised historical pageants, in which the staff took part. Marjorie Beasley, left, represented 1934, probably the year that the photograph was taken. Her colleague Flora Clarke was 1785, the year in which Edmund Cartwright built the first successful power-loom.

Below: Clayton Hall Grammar School under-15s netball team after what appears to have been a successful 1969/70 season. Lining up behind centre and captain Susan Guest are, from left to right: Ruth Burgess, Susan Goodwin, Carol Mothershaw, Mavis Cairns and sisters Margaret and Susan Platt.

four
In Uniform

Above: St George's Church Lads Brigade, holding their carbines, line up behind the Brunswick Chapel in School Street in around 1906. Formed at the turn of the twentieth century at the time of the Second Boer War, they first paraded at Queen Victoria's memorial service in 1901. The arrival of the charismatic Revd Albert Baines (fifth from the right) in 1905 led to an increase in numbers, but following the First World War interest declined and the group eventually disbanded.

Left: Staffordshire Rifle Volunteers at the time of the Second Boer War; kneeling on the right is bugler and marksman Enoch Shufflebotham of Hassall Street. He later ran a painting and decorating business and became a lieutenant in St George's Church Lads Brigade. Serving in the First World War with the 7th Battalion North Staffords, he was fatally wounded by a sniper in Mesopotamia and is remembered on the Basra War Memorial and in St Paul's Church.

The Staffordshire Yeomanry Cavalry, part of the Territorial Force, holding a religious service during their 1911 summer camp at Keele Park. The Yeomanry, with a Newcastle troop commanded by Colonel Earl Gower of Trentham Hall, was formed in 1794 in response to the threat from Napoleon. In their early days they guarded prisoners, helped control crowds during periods of civil unrest and formed escorts on ceremonial occasions.

A group of well-turned-out Army Cadet Force members affiliated to the North Staffordshire Regiment stand to attention for Chesterton photographer Mr Barnard during the First World War. The picture was probably taken at the National School in Church Street, Chesterton. Officer Training Corps units and ACF detachments like this one were very popular during the First World War and were formed almost everywhere.

Royal Army Service Corps recruits at Butterton Hall near Newcastle are pictured in this postcard, sent by one of them to his daughter in June 1915. In September 1914 the newly formed 2nd/5th Battalion North Staffordshire Regiment set up headquarters at the hall, leaving in February 1915, to be followed by the RASC. Damage caused by the military occupation of the hall was probably a factor in its later demolition.

The First World War army recruits training at Butterton Hall could purchase cigarettes, matches and similar items in the camp canteen seen here. Liquid refreshment seems to have been limited to a glass of beer or a mug of tea or cocoa. Skerratts ran a newspaper stall at the camp and the YMCA tent provided somewhere to spend off-duty hours playing cards and dominoes.

All the marching and drilling at Butterton Hall must have created large appetites judging by the scene in the back room of the canteen, where large quantities of bacon rashers are piled up next to the slicer. On the table military-sized loaves, marked BA & Co., were probably baked by Boyce Adams' Hanley bakery. There are also large tins of Archer's Helmet Brand Corned Beef and yet more sides of bacon.

Newcastle Church Lads Brigade boys, probably from St George's Church, seen at the King's Royal Rifle Corps camp at Llandudno in 1923. A battalion of the KRRC was formed entirely of current and former members of the CLB by their commandant Field-Marshall Lord Grenfell, which may account for their presence at the camp. From left to right: C. Shufflebotham, F. Brown, T. Davis, ? Bailey and E. Shufflebotham.

BOROUGH OF NEWCASTLE-UNDER LYME.

Police Notice.

RAIDS by AIRCRAFT.

In the event of information being received at the Police Station of the probability of an Air Raid on the district in the night time, instructions may be issued for Gas and Electricity to be turned off at the respective Works. The Electric Light will be turned on again as soon as the danger is considered to be over, but the Gas, if cut off completely, will not be turned on again until Nine o'clock next morning. In the event of such an extreme step being taken as the complete cutting off of the Gas supply, inhabitants are requested next morning to rouse any of their neighbours who are in the habit of leaving any gas jets burning all night and sleeping late in the mornings. Such cases might occur especially with elderly people or in cases of sickness.

Pending the consideration of the advisability of the compulsory restriction of lighting in the town, the public are requested to reduce the light both in shops and private houses as much as possible, and to use dark blinds or heavy curtains, and where gas is used not to leave a light burning during the night unless absolutely necessary.

In the event of an Air Raid occurring in the Borough, the public are advised that the safest place is in the cellars; assembling in the streets only increases the danger.

Persons ringing up the Police Station for news at the time of an expected Air Raid need not be surprised if they are unceremoniously cut off. When anything of this kind is expected and public enquiries by telephone are constantly arriving at the Police Station, much valuable time is sometimes lost by attending to them, in addition to the wire being monopolised when required for other urgent and important messages.

WILLIAM FORSTER,

Chief Constable's Office,
Police Station,
Newcastle, Staffs.,
3rd February, 1916.

CHIEF CONSTABLE.

G. T. BAGGULEY, PRINTER, NEWCASTLE.

Left: There must have been a strong expectation of attack from the air in First World War Newcastle, as the chief constable took the rather draconian measures outlined on this poster. Most of the inhabitants would probably have been more concerned at the possibility of the gas being turned off without warning and being switched on again the following morning while they were still asleep.

Below: At the end of the First World War this Mark IV Male tank was presented to the borough in recognition of its contribution to the war effort. It stood for over twenty years in Stubbs Walks, but was removed for scrap at the beginning of the Second World War. One of around 2,350 tanks made during the war, this one, fitted with cannon, bears the number 151, indicating that it was used for training purposes.

War memorials sprang up in many parts of Newcastle after the First World War, including this one, erected by the people of Knutton and seen at its dedication ceremony. It stood near St Mary's Church at the junction of Knutton and Church Lanes. Those from Knutton who died in the Second World War were added to the back of the memorial and it was later turned around and moved a short distance to its present position by Knutton Clinic.

These three sergeants from the Betley Home Guard are typical of the many former First World War soldiers and other volunteers who organised themselves into an effective home defence force in the Newcastle area during the Second World War. On the left is Sgt Joe Edwards, for many years a miner at Leycett Colliery, who was promoted to company sergeant-major by the end of the war, and on the right is Sgt Joe Birchall.

Early in 1940 the British Thomson-Houston Co. Ltd built a factory in Lower Milehouse Lane to produce anti-aircraft shells for the Admiralty. By the end of the war the factory had produced twenty million shells and ten million igniters; part of the two-pounder shell production line is shown here. BTH retained the factory after the war, making electric motors, and it was only demolished at the beginning of 2005.

The British Thomson-Houston Co. Ltd munitions factory formed its own team of volunteer firefighters to protect the buildings and personnel from the consequences of air raids and accidents. The team pictured here includes Percy Leech (front row on the right), who worked at BTH for many years and was also a well-known lay preacher on the Methodist circuit in the Newcastle area.

Left: A group of Second World War volunteer air-raid precaution wardens and fire watchers from the Chesterton and Bradwell area, including Beryl Downing in the middle and Bradwell Hospital matron Eva Wilson on the right. They stand in front of an anti-blast wall of sandbags protecting the entrance to a building, possibly Bradwell Hospital, and have a bucket of water, a stirrup pump, gas masks and hurricane lamps on hand.

Below: This wartime group photographed outside Bradwell Lodge with their mobile pump is the Wolstanton Auxiliary Fire Service (AFS) team, displaying a trophy they had won in an exercise. The AFS, formed in 1938, had the task of putting out blazes caused by German incendiary devices. Even today unexploded examples of these bombs occasionally turn up lodged in roofs. Front right is Edward Shone, who was a full-time firefighter.

This group of Newcastle firemen proudly display a trophy they have won in a competition. The initials NFS on their uniforms stands for National Fire Service, which was formed in 1941. This amalgamation of the regular fire brigades and the volunteer Auxiliary Fire Service took place to provide a nationwide organisation of firefighting personnel during the Second World War. On the left is Edward Shone.

Annual inspection day at Newcastle High School in May 1952. The school's Combined Cadet Force lines up for an inspection by Brigadier L.N. Tyler from the War Office, with headmaster James Todd and commanding officer Lt-Col. J.P.C. Smith. School cadets were originally part of the Officer Training Corps, formed in 1908, which later became known as the Junior Training Corps and in 1948 as the Combined Cadet Force.

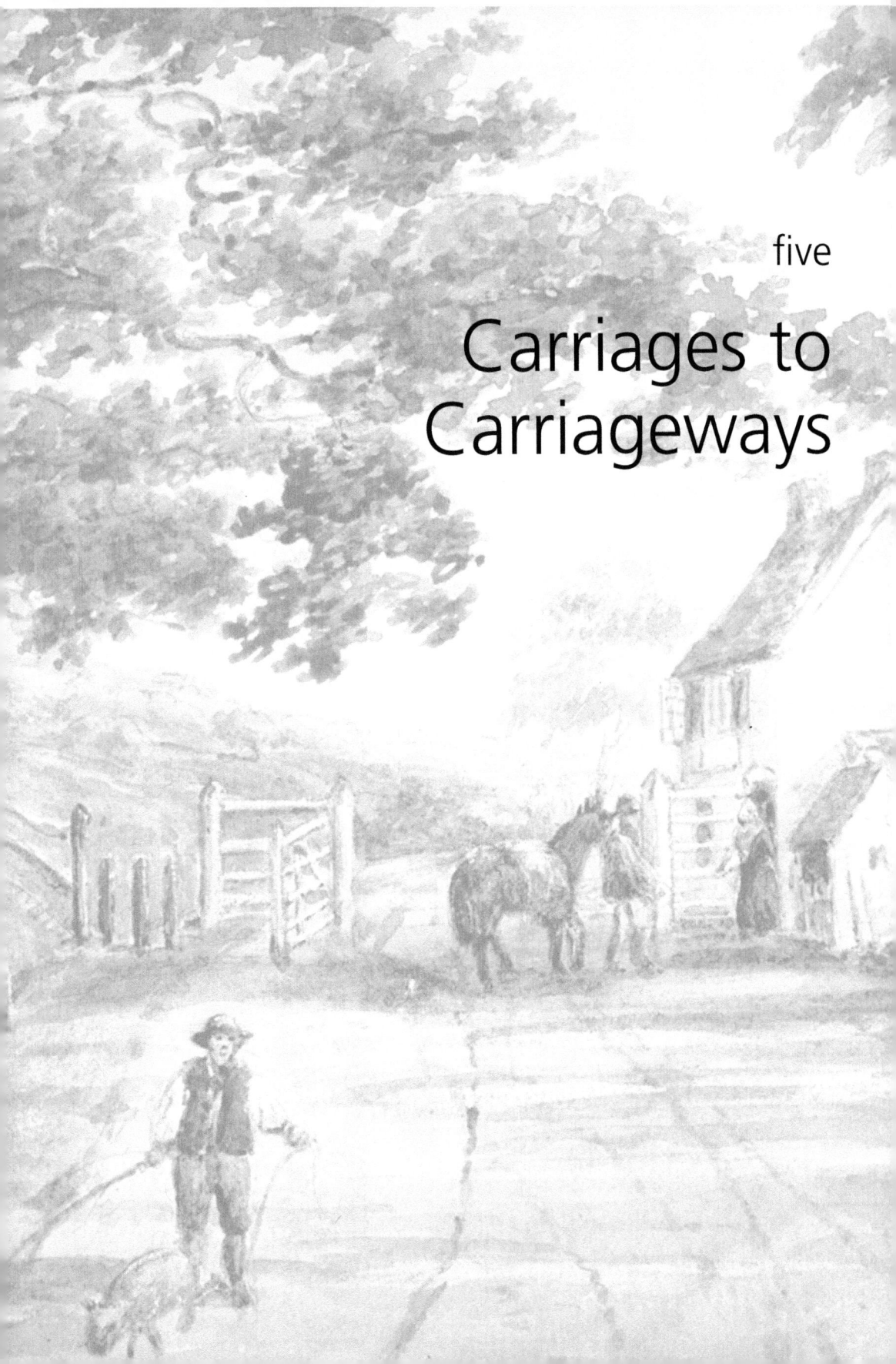

five

Carriages to Carriageways

This watercolour of Dimsdale toll gate was possibly painted by Mary Smith in around 1860. In the eighteenth and nineteenth centuries investors would pay for the 'turnpiking' of sections of road and would then receive a share of the toll paid by everyone passing through the 'bar'. In 1871 the toll gate keeper here was Thomas Beasley, whose great-granddaughter Marjorie represents 1934 on page 34.

This postcard from around 1910 shows the same scene as the painting above. Despite the passage of half a century, the only major difference is the absence of the toll gate. The road is now the four-lane A34 dual carriageway between Mile House roundabout and Dimsdale Parade. The toll house is long gone, replaced by the Stop Inn Motel.

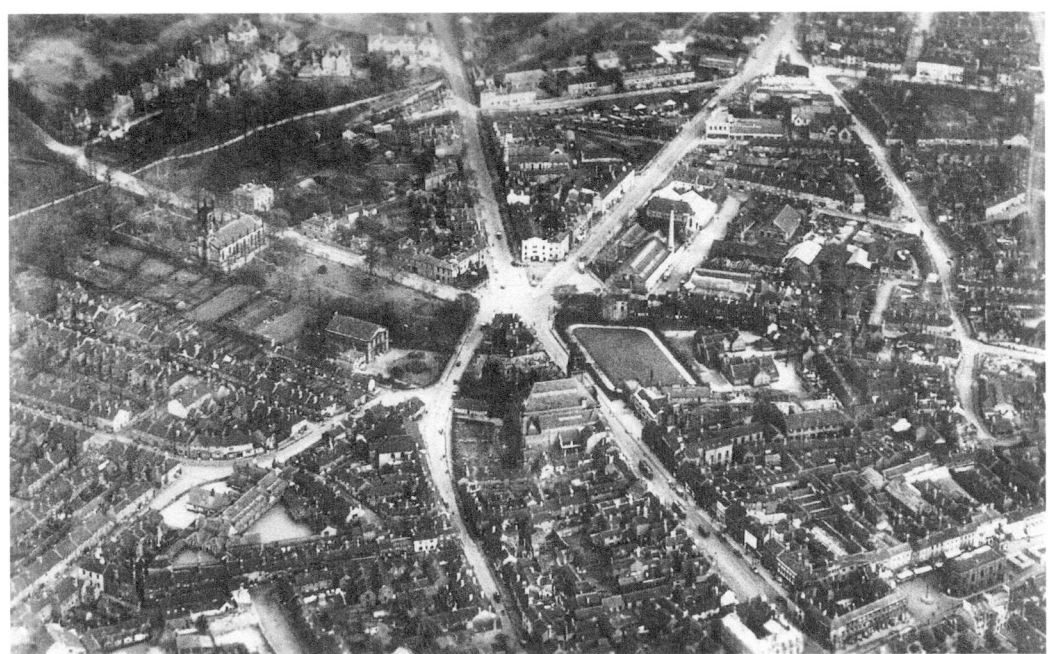

This 1930s aerial view shows the massive changes which would be imposed on Newcastle by the diversion of the A34 bypass. Clearly visible are the eighteenth-century roads radiating from Nelson Place, formerly an area of marshland. Although the A34 itself is not shown, the extent of clearance required to connect Nelson Place to it is obvious. Today's carriageways now dwarf all of the roads shown here.

The construction of the A34 diversion resulted in hundreds of properties being demolished and residential areas such as Upper and Lower Green disappearing entirely, after being in existence since the twelfth century. Other buildings visible here would disappear later; Holborn paper mill was destroyed by fire, the Dog & Partridge was demolished and the tall buildings in Red Lion Square were cleared to make way for the York Place shopping precinct.

High Street in 1965. Work on the Grosvenor roundabout is well underway and the buildings to the left of the Spread Eagle await their fate. On either side of Bernard's painters and decorators were what will probably prove to be the last ever private houses on Newcastle's main street. Today only public house living accommodation and a few flats can be found within the ring of dual carriageways encircling the town centre.

All the buildings here would soon make way for the A34 diversion. No longer would heavy lorries negotiate High Street's market stalls, but instead would move freely along the dual carriageway following the course of Holborn, Lower Street and part of Goose Street. The digger is beginning the excavation of the Grosvenor 'sunken' roundabout which originally boasted a fountain, although this was soon converted into a flowerbed.

Three of the shops in Liverpool Road demolished at the time the new carriageway was punched through from Nelson Place to the A34 ring road. Although its neighbours were empty, Bickley's tools had not yet finished moving their stock to new premises. Demolished at the same time were the premises which had housed the Harrison family's photography business from 1873 until around 1960.

This longer view shows the positions of the three shops above in relation to buildings still standing today. Beyond the roadworks on the left is Lyme Street (now Corporation Street), and beyond that is Salters Lane, now much shortened and re-named Hickman Street. Brian Smith's jewellers moved with Bickley's to new premises at the top of Bridge Street and in 2005 is finally closing.

Holborn, photographed by Thomas Wantling of the Dog & Partridge in around 1964. Holborn was once lined on both sides by houses, shops and pubs, but soon after this photograph was taken the 'Dog', the only survivor, would be overshadowed by the new A34 bypass. Today five lanes of dual carriageway pass over this spot and a large roundabout occupies the high ground to the north, formerly part of Upper Green.

The construction of the A34 dual carriageway between Lower Street and Upper Green in 1965. The new road, much higher than Holborn, is being levelled to produce a smooth incline between the roundabouts at either end. Holborn would eventually be less than half its width here and the Dog & Partridge (on the extreme right) would survive only until the 1970s before being demolished.

six

A World Apart

This etching of Maer Hall appeared in *The Builder* in the 1890s, praising the fine workmanship in the extensions commissioned by shipowner Frederick Harrison. The joinery was the work of Thomas Edwards of Ironmarket, later Jones-Moss. The magnificent staircase still survives, although sadly without its lion lamps and today cut into sections, one in Ebenezer House in Newcastle and the other in Market Drayton, in a house allegedly modelled around it.

This 1940s photograph shows Maer Hall's Victorian extensions from the churchyard of St Peter's. The relationship between hall and church is unusual here, in that from the churchyard it is very easy to overlook the hall and its gardens. It was not unusual for country house owners to have entire villages moved to prevent them being visible from the house. At this time the Misses Harrison would still have been in residence.

The courtyard at Keele Hall, by Harrison. Entering the hall via the main entrance, visible through the open gate, involves ascending a number of steps both inside and out, definitely unsuitable for wheelchair access. Above the door is the muniment room, where important family documents were kept. This has an oriel window above the coat of arms of Queen Elizabeth I. The tower, altered during the 1860s rebuilding, houses the grand staircase.

Above: Keele Hall after 1888, when Colonel Ralph Sneyd, last of his line, had added his gun room to the far corner of the south front. Sneyd was seldom at Keele, preferring to spend his time in London or overseas, often amongst royalty. The changes he made at Keele reflected his sporting interests; new gun and billiard rooms, and an entire racecourse and stud farm constructed in the park, served by its own railway station.

Left: Another Harrison study, showing the Great Hall's fireplace surrounded by family portraits. The arms, made up of forty-two quarterings, show the Sneyd arms in first and last place with the arms of heiresses who married into the family between them. Despite its magnificent fireplace, the hall is surprisingly small, measuring only 36ft by 26ft, although the fact that it rises 30ft through two floors gives an atmosphere of great spaciousness.

This wintry scene shows members of the Keele Hall outdoor staff in the 'Pleasure Grounds'. Behind them is the holly hedge, believed to be around 235 years old. Sadly only parts of this now survive and they are, like the grounds generally, suffering from a lack of attention. In 1891, not including gardeners, gamekeepers or other outdoor servants, Keele employed thirty-two staff to attend to a family of just four.

Seabridge Hall, *c.* 1905. This building seems to excite little interest amongst local historians and is seldom mentioned in local publications. At the time this picture was taken the hall had been inhabited for many years by Arthur Price Llewellyn, a prestigious solicitor occupying many influential positions, including secretary to the British Pottery Manufacturers Federation. Before Llewellyn, timber merchant James Hall had lived there for at least ten years.

Above: This 1960s view of the Clayton Lodge Hotel shows the Georgian house with three bays, built in around 1805, which is today at the centre of a motley assemblage of buildings. The roof was altered and the turret and bay window added around the turn of the twentieth century, and the extension on the right with bay and oriel windows was probably built in around 1920 by G.H. 'Harry' Downing, head of the tile-manufacturing firm.

Left: Samuel John Stone in around 1890, whose best works have remained well-known into the twenty-first century. Stone wrote around fifty hymns, including 'The Church's One Foundation', for which the music *Aurelia* was written by Samuel Wesley, great-nephew of the founder of Methodism. Stone was born in 1839 in Whitmore, where his father was curate, although the family later moved to Butterton and then to Clayton Lodge during the 1840s.

Betley has always been amply provided with gentleman's residences. Betley Hall was completed in 1783 for Charles and Catherine Tollett, who previously lived at Betley Court. It overlooked an enlarged ornamental lake which fed a wtaermill near to timber-framed Betley Old Hall, which still stands today. Confusingly, a seventeenth-century Betley New Hall was demolished when this hall was built. From the 1930s until the 1970s this house was simply left to decay.

This large lake is still in existence but is easy to miss, despite its proximity to the main Keele-Nantwich Road. The lake was extended in a round 1770 to improve the setting of the hall and provide an adequate supply of water for the nearby meadows and mill. More recently, luxury homes have been built on the banks and for a time one of these was occupied by a certain Robbie Williams.

Left: Although few today recognise his name, Captain Ewart Scott Grogan was one of the most outstanding people to have lived in the borough. 'Cape-to-Cairo' Grogan was the first person to make an overland crossing of Africa, an escapade which nearly cost him his life on several occasions. A cross between Indiana Jones and Dr Livingstone, Grogan lived at Camp Hill, Maer Hills between 1908 and 1914 and stood for Parliament in Newcastle twice in 1910.

Below: The Drawing Room at Camp Hill, *c.* 1914. Grogan stood as Newcastle's Unionist candidate in the two tempestuous General Elections of 1910, losing twice to Josiah Clement Wedgwood, a direct relative of Camp Hill's builder. Grogan, in Africa when the second election was called, travelled 6,000 miles to spend just one day campaigning and still came a very respectable second. The name 'Grogan' can be seen painted on the base of the right-hand tusk.

This view of Butterton Hall is unusual, having been taken from the rear and from the opposite side to every other known photograph. For this reason the photograph provides valuable information about the range of buildings to the left. Sadly the Pilkington family archive at Wakefield does not contain any photographs of Butterton Hall, but it does include some maps and improvement plans for the Butterton Estate.

Although living outside the borough, the Leveson-Gower's (pronounced Loosen-Gore) of Trentham Hall owned the majority of Newcastle properties in the eighteenth century and controlled the town's two parliamentary seats for over a century. This photograph does not really do justice to Charles Barry's Italianate palace, of which only the entrance wing in the foreground, the church and the state apartments (visible to the far right of the main block) still stand today.

Dimsdale Hall during demolition, *c.* 1920. This sixteenth-century building would in its heyday have rivalled most in the area. It was the home of the Brett family, which included knights, Mayors of Newcastle and Justices of the Peace for Staffordshire. Just visible to the right of the roof is part of the later Dutch-style brick frontage. Today only the barn on the left survives.

Part of the brick façade added to the timber-framed Dimsdale Hall, seen during demolition. This photograph was taken on the same day as the previous one and soon only this frontage would remain standing. The hall was located in the wooded area just behind Wolstanton Golf Club's club house. The old barn with its stone-mullioned windows has recently undergone conversion into a house.

seven

Class of
their own

St Giles & St George's National School began as St Giles' School in Bagnall Street, now part of Barracks Road, in 1826. It merged with St George's Infant School, founded in 1835, during a period of reorganisation in the Newcastle schools system in the 1870s. These girls from the school had been successful in obtaining scholarships to the Orme Girls School in 1926.

This picture of Class 1 and 2 girls at St Giles & St George's National School was taken in around 1885 by a travelling photographer from Chesterfield. Edith and Ethel Beresford, daughters of Eli and Susan Beresford (then living in George Street), are in the third row back on the right. Ethel later became the matron of the Newcastle Almhouses and is shown as an elderly lady there on page 72.

Boys at Chesterton National School in the 1870s. The school was founded in 1814 and rebuilt when Chesterton became a parish in 1846. A separate girls school was added in 1855. On the back row, the third boy from the left is Amos Taylor of Apedale Road, Chesterton. On leaving he became a teacher at the school and went on to marry Bertha Downing, before becoming a partner in Downing's brickworks.

The Standard IV girls of St Giles & St George's in 1921 look quite different from their Victorian forebears on the previous page. In 1948 the school became a mixed junior and senior school, the seniors finally moving to other schools in 1966. Mrs Audrey Lawton, who loaned both photographs, is in the third row back, fifth from the right, aged eight; she is the niece of Edith and Ethel Beresford.

Grammar school education came to Newcastle as early as 1602 when Richard Clayton left £10 per annum for the teaching of thirty children by a master. Further bequests followed and by the 1860s it was recognised that new schools were required. As a result the Endowed Schools Trust opened Newcastle High School for Boys in April 1874, moving into the newly built school on Stubbs Field in 1876.

The assembly hall at Newcastle High School, shown here in around 1900. It was known as 'Big School', one of a number of indicators that the first headmaster, Mr F.E. Kitchener, had come from Rugby School. Generous gifts from Joseph Mayer, a former pupil of the old Newcastle Grammar School who had lived at Thistleberry House and made his fortune as a Liverpool goldsmith, helped provide paintings for the hall.

Joseph Mayer also established scholarships in several subjects at the school which continue to this day, and provided the nucleus of the school library, shown in this early photograph. His contribution to the library included folios of the original correspondence of the famous potter Josiah Wedgwood, as well as historical and antiquarian exhibits for the school museum.

Despite a main emphasis on academic achievement, Newcastle High School did not forget the importance of gaining manual skills; all pupils received a grounding in woodwork and metalwork in the workshops, originally opened in 1887. Here Mr Terry Williams supervises a young pupil learning to machine on a lathe, watched closely by his classmates. Mr Williams, now retired, has recently had his first novel published.

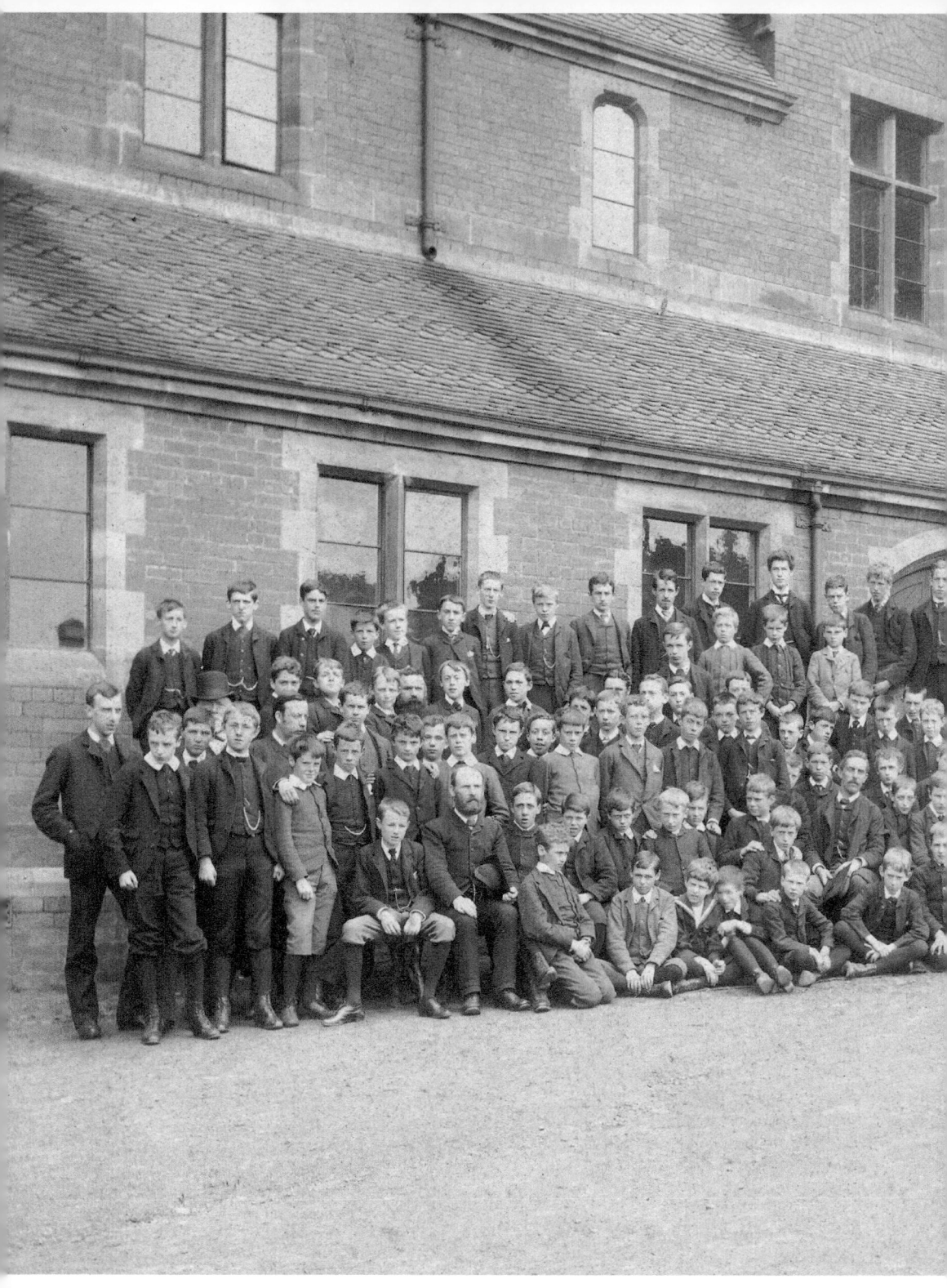

This early picture of the boys at Newcastle High School was taken in the old quadrangle in the late 1890s, before any building alterations occurred. The headmaster was Mr G.W. Rundall and he and the bearded former

headmaster Mr F.E. Kitchener can be seen seated towards the centre of the picture. Mr Kitchener become chairman of the governors in 1896 and remained closely involved in school affairs up until his death in 1915.

This early picture shows the Orme Charity School, opened in 1851 on the site of the old workhouse on the Higherland. It offered a better standard of education than the existing elementary schools. In 1872 it became the Middle School for Boys, closing in 1928 when teachers and pupils moved to the newly built Wolstanton Grammar School. The school reopened in 1931 as the Orme Boys County Secondary School.

'All work and no play makes Jack a dull boy' says the old dictum, but it is difficult to identify 'Jack' with most children in costume at the Betley School Annual Fancy Dress Dance in the school hall on 9 February 1932. Country dancing took place under the guidance of schoolteacher Miss Jones to the accompaniment of Miss Challinor's Band from Leycett. Betley School celebrated its 150th anniversary in 2004.

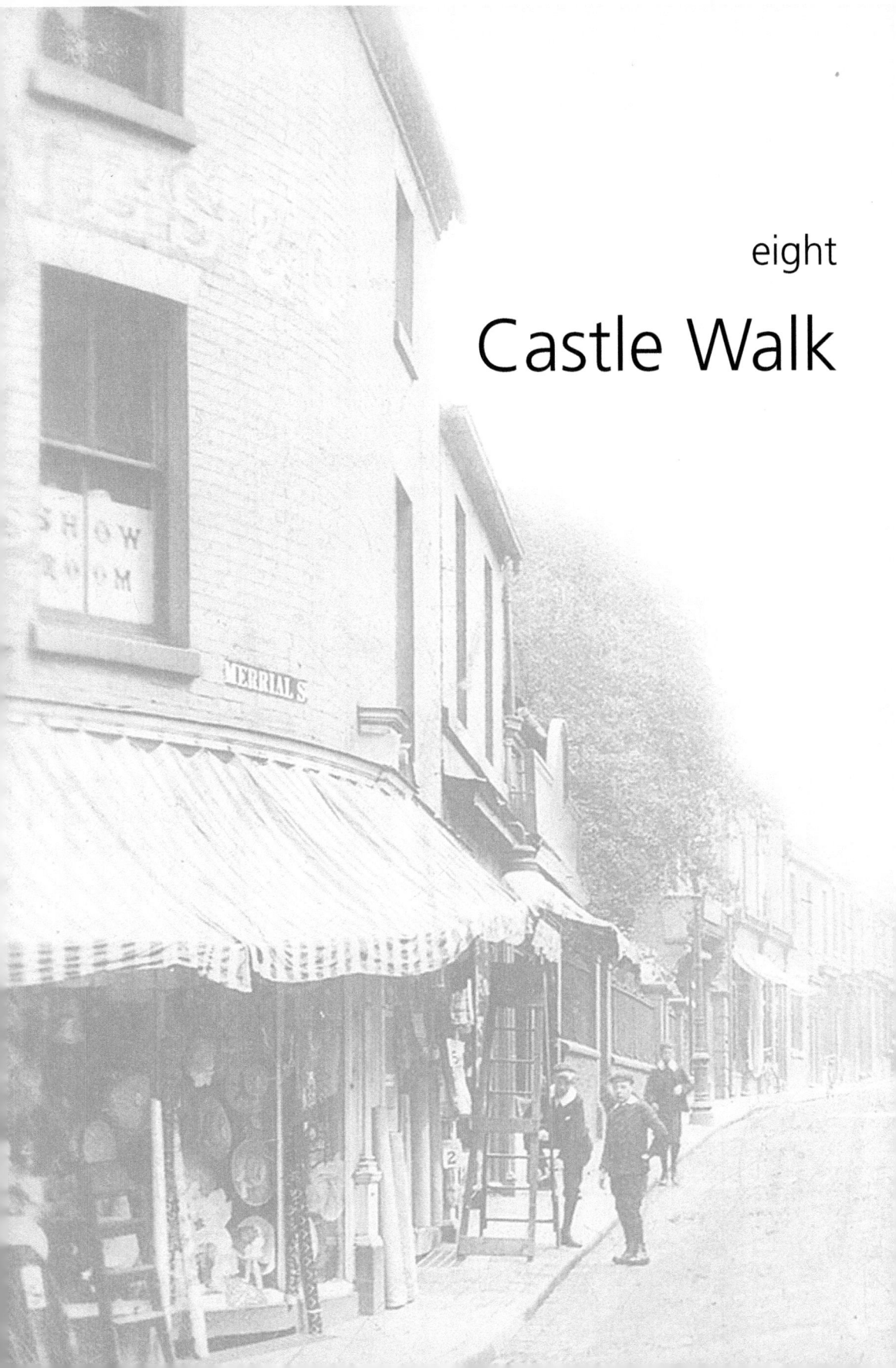

eight

Castle Walk

St Giles' Church overlooks Red Lion Square in around 1905 as groups of children watch the photographer. The Weights and Measures Office stands in the middle of the Square and to the left is Beeston's Vaults, an old coaching inn, separated from Phoenix's confectioners by Pepper Street. The timber-framed building further along houses the Three Tuns Inn and Charles Rennat's Gentlemens Outfitters. On the right is Wain's Chemist.

Clement Wain's was a familiar sight in Red Lion Square from the late 1890s, in premises previously occupied by grocer William Rimell. Wain's later took over the adjoining shop to sell camera and cine equipment. Around the corner, Mrs Wheat's Tobacconists opened just before Wain's. Mrs Wheat was the wife of Daniel Wheat, Inspector of Nuisances to the Local Health Board, and they lived in London Road.

Right: John Godwin, printer, stationer and newsagent, occupied the shop next to Wain's, previously owned by draper John McKee. Godwin had taken over the business from a relative in around 1885, having previously been a railway stationmaster in Burslem. The newspaper placards outside announce the success of the Hon. C.S. Rolls' (of Rolls-Royce) cross-channel flight on 2 June 1910. Sadly Rolls died in an aircraft accident the following month.

Below: Merrial Street from Red Lion Square (*c.* 1910) with the Central Hotel on the right and Wilding's drapery shop to the left. The Central was previously called the Happy Land Inn and had been a popular beerhouse since at least 1850. The hotel and other buildings on the same side were replaced by the York Place shopping centre in around 1968, and Merrial Street was widened.

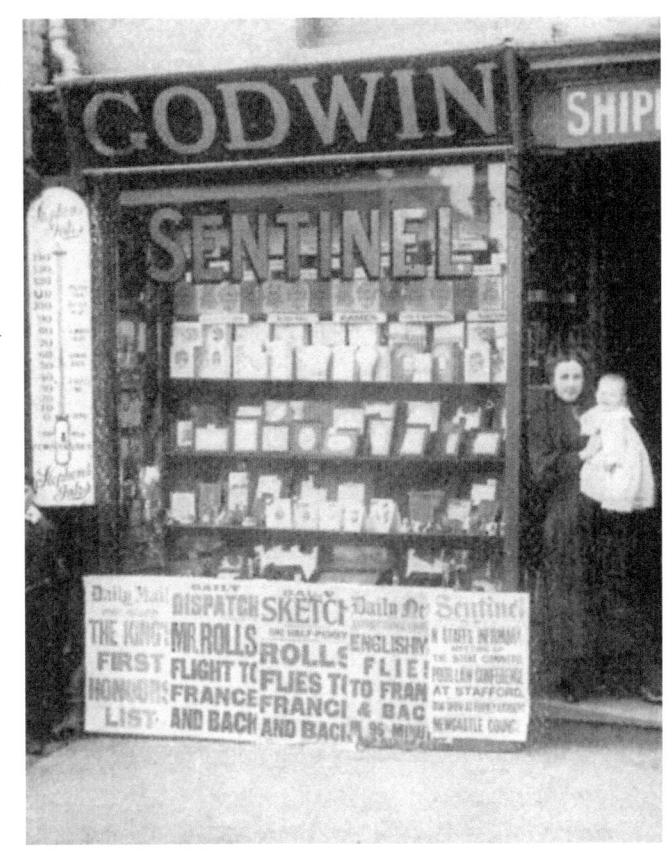

Newcastle Almshouses, at the junction of Bridge Street and Lower Green, were built with a bequest left by the 2nd Duke of Albemarle who died in 1688. His heirs, the Leveson-Gowers of Trentham Hall, carried out his wishes in 1743 accommodating twenty widows. Allowances for maintenance and blue cloth for gowns to be worn in public, along with the right to choose inmates and trustees were enshrined in the agreement.

Control of Newcastle Almshouses passed to Newcastle Council in 1940 following an agreement with the Duke of Sutherland, and they were then sold to the Ministry of Transport. New premises were to be built prior to the original property's demolition, but this did not actually occur until 1964. Here we see some of the widows at the rear of the building in around 1950 with the matron, Miss Ethel Beresford, seated on the left.

At 5 Bridge Street in around 1905 Thomas Caddy, fruiterer and florist, had a splendid array of items for sale, from bananas to potted palms. Caddy also had a large fruit and vegetable stall in Market Place, opposite the Guildhall. He later moved from Bridge Street to premises in Penkhull Street. The window of Oxen's Chemists, across the road, can be seen reflected in the glass.

Oxen's in Bridge Street replaced the shop front reflected in Caddy's window with this less ornate one, seen here in 1910. They claimed to have the largest stock of patent medicines and toilet articles in North Staffordshire. 'Juno's Indian Drops' cured wind and other unmentionable ailments, while 'Spraggox' remedied neuralgia and nerves. They opened a second shop in High Street next to Mandley & Unett's in around 1905.

Left: Prominently sited at the end of Merrial Street were drapers Wilding & Co., who had taken over the business of Rees Jones & Co. in around 1905. Wilding's also had a second shop in High Street and, according to a contemporary advertisement, their stock included ladies' and children's underclothing, hosiery, trimmings, gloves and hats. The premises shown are now occupied by Butters' Estate Agents.

Below: A mixture of Georgian and Victorian buildings on the left side of Merrial Street (*c.* 1967) are mostly empty and awaiting demolition. To the left is Harry Stephens' greengrocers, then Edward Prince Fashions, Bookland, Massey's leather goods and Hulse, the house furnishers, who later moved to the bottom of Merrial Street on the opposite side. Fred Brown's Cycles was located on the right beyond the Conservative Club.

Left: The Globe Hotel and Commercial Inn in Red Lion Square was a coaching inn and posting house with 'excellent stabling and well-aired beds'. It was replaced in 1898 by this substantial ornate red-brick building of the same name, built by Samuel Wilton. Seen here in the mid-1960s, it was being used as temporary premises by Bookland. Next door was Craddock's shoe shop, founded by the Craddock brothers in around 1890.

Below: The Globe Hotel in the final stages of demolition in 1967. To the right, Craddock's shoe shop and Otet's television shop await the same fate. The area was being cleared to make way for the proposed York Place pedestrian shopping centre, including up to thirty-one shops. Craddock's reopened in the new building, between Bookland and Blood Lloyd's record shop, close to its original position.

Robert Beresford opened the Pavilion cinema in 1922, complete with bicycle and radio shops and petrol pumps on the pavement. The premises had previously been the Central Motor Garage. The first 'talkies' were shown here in 1929 and the Regal cinema was added in 1931. Mayor of Newcastle three times,

Beresford played a key role in preventing Newcastle and Wolstanton becoming part of Stoke-on-Trent in 1930. He died aged fifty-six in 1936.

Bagguley's High Street premises on the left became part of the adjoining Henry White's ladies shop, Sutherland House, in 1952. A plain building until the Ionic columns were added in around 1930, it had originally been The Roebuck, the largest coaching inn in Newcastle. The Leveson-Gowers kept it to maintain their influence in local politics when the old Roebuck opposite became too small for the purpose.

Substantial changes took place in the 1980s with the construction of the Roebuck shopping centre behind the shop fronts seen above. The visual impact on High Street of such a large retail development was lessened by the retention of the old façades. To bridge the gap over the entrance seen in this picture, the Ionic columns on Sutherland House were increased in number from five to nine.

Above: This view of Ironmarket, photographed in around 1926, is not quite what it seems. It has been 'modernised' to make the scene look like it was taken in the early 1930s, to obtain further postcard sales from the image. The tramlines have been removed, a tram coming up behind PET bus EH 6003 erased and buildings beyond the tram painted in. It would surely have been easier just to take another photograph!

Left: Alexander Bayley already owned this Ironmarket catering and confectionery business, seen here in 1910, when in 1871 he took over the Roebuck Mews in High Street, offering 'horses, carriages and funeral equipages'. The Roebuck coaching inn, with its own blacksmiths and stabling for seventy-four horses, was by then being converted into shops. By 1900 Bayley was also running the Castle Hotel and Restaurant on High Street.

A civic procession moving down Ironmarket in the 1950s passes Jones Moss & Co. house furnishers and the George & Dragon public house. The headteachers of the endowed schools follow precedent by walking before the macebearers and the high constable. Mr James Todd from Newcastle High School is on the right and members of the school's Combined Cadet Force line the roadside.

Miss A.B. Hobbis, milliner, costumier and fancy draper, operated a genteel establishment from the ground floor of a large townhouse adjoining the Municipal Hall. Seen here in around 1910, it supplied wedding outfits, trousseaux and mourning orders. Specialities included bridesmaids hats, exclusively designed French blouses, 'dainty' lingerie and the feather boas seen hanging in the left-hand window.

Batte's high-class fruiterers and florist shop in part of the Star Inn, Ironmarket, used the wider pavements there to display produce outside. They were able to provide 'wreaths, crosses and bouquets on the shortest notice' when required. Samuel Batte, previously a Wolverhampton shoe dealer, began as a fishmonger and fruiterer in Friars Street. This shop was run by his daughter Violet while his eldest son Roland looked after the stalls on the 'Stones'.

In 1935 Newcastle celebrated the 700th anniversary of King Henry III's charter confirming the town as a free borough and establishing a guild merchant. This display in the Queen's Gardens formed part of the decorations put up in the town for the event. The words 'Progress 1235-1935' were symbolised by the castle and an aeroplane, and the areas of improvement underlined by the signs for Housing and Education.

Above: The Municipal Hall in Ironmarket, seen here from Queen's Gardens (*c.* 1935), was built to commemorate Queen Victoria's Golden Jubilee in 1887 and was completed in 1890. It was built on the site of Arlington House, purchased by the Corporation from the Newcastle MP William S. Allen. It provided the town with a large public hall and council chamber and shortly afterwards housed the library and art school.

Left: This close-up of the front of the Municipal Hall gives some idea of the richness of its ornamentation and detail, with red brick contrasting with the stone dressings. Two of the four life-size statues representing architecture, painting, music and literature can be seen here. Its 'Flemish'-style architecture may not have appealed to everyone, but its demolition in 1967 was a substantial loss to town centre amenities.

Opposite: This original poster advertises the Famous Minstrel Mites as a forthcoming attraction at the Municipal Hall in February 1893. Live entertainment in Newcastle had previously taken place in the Royal Theatre in Nelson Place, the Guildhall, church halls and venues such as Marsh Street Lecture Hall, where the Minstrel Mites had already appeared in 1891. The price of admission was 3d, 6d or 1s, although reserved seats cost 1s 6d.

MUNICIPAL HALL
NEWCASTLE.

FOR 3 NIGHTS ONLY,
SATURDAY, MONDAY & TUESDAY
February 18th, 20th and 21st, 1893.

The only Genuine CHILDREN'S TROUPE in the World—

THE
MINSTREL
MITES

Proprietors - - Messrs. H. Hayward & J. Davis

New Wardrobe, New Scenery, New Songs, New Dances, New Com'calities. IN FACT—Everything New for this Season!

Above: Nelson Place was the setting for the royal visit, on 22 April 1913, of King George V and Queen Mary, seen here on the dais with the Mayor of Newcastle William Mellard and other dignitaries. The royal party's tour of towns and factories in North Staffordshire caused great excitement both in Newcastle and the surrounding area and the streets were lavishly decorated with flags and bunting for the occasion.

Left: An earlier royal presence in Nelson Place was the statue of Queen Victoria, presented by Sir Alfred Seale Haslam MP during his third term as Newcastle's mayor. It was unveiled with great ceremony on 5 November 1903 by the Lord High Steward of Newcastle, His Imperial Highness the Grand Duke Michael of Russia. Removed to obscurity in Station Walks in 1963, the statue now stands more appropriately in Queen's Gardens.

Right: Rupert Simms, book dealer and author, was born at Consall Forge in 1853, moving to Silverdale in 1863 after losing both his hands in a brickworks accident the previous year. Working first as a tea hawker, by 1881 he was living in Friars Street selling books in the nearby Market Hall. In 1883 he began to compile material for his memorable county bibliography *Bibliotheca Staffordiensis*, published in 1894.

Below: By 1900 Simms had moved to this shop in Ironmarket, near the Compasses Inn. The shop appears to have been run by his wife Mary and offered 'the best and fairest prices for what you have to sell'. Now working as a commission agent as well as selling books and prints, Simms retired from business in 1932 and died aged eighty-five in August 1937.

Nelson Place and King Street in around 1905, with the Royal Theatre in its original form on the right. A group of local businessmen, including Josiah Wedgwood and Josiah Spode, leased a plot of reclaimed land there from the Marsh Trustees to build the theatre. It was built in 1787/88 by architect and builder John Pepper, who lived in what is now Mayer House in nearby Queen Street.

After falling into disuse the Royal Theatre was given a new façade in 1910 and reopened as the Cinema Theatre. Billed as Newcastle's first picture house, it became the Plaza in 1930 when purchased by Robert Beresford, the Roxy in 1946 and finally closed in 1957. Several other Newcastle cinemas opened around this time, including the King's Hall in High Street and the Tivoli in Church Street.

A PLAY and Farce, never acted here.

For the BENEFIT of

Mrs. Norman.

Who with due deference informs the Ladies and Gentlemen of Newcastle and the POTTERIES, and their vicinity, that she has procured a correct Copy of the PLAY as it is now performing with universal applause, at the Theat: Royal Covent Garden; and humbly hopes it will merit their approbation & patronage,

Newcastle and Pottery Theatre.

On Monday Evening Decr. 31st,

Will be presented, that NEW popular PLAY of

Lovers Vows:

OR, THE

Natural Son.

This favorite piece is the production of the celebrated KOTZBUE, Author the "Stranger" &c.—Translated from the German by Mrs Inchbald, which originality of language and incident is allowed to be the criterion of the pro Drama,

Baron Wildenhaim	— — —	Mr	PATTERSO
Count Caffel	— — —	Mr	SHERIDEN
Anhalt	— — —	Mr	LOYD
Frederick	— — —	Mr	FULLERTON
Verdun (the Butter)	— —	Mr	NORMAN
Landlord	— —	Mr	WELCH
Cottager	— —	Mr	RICHARDSON
Farmer	— —	Mr	HUME
Agatha Friburgh	— — —	Mrs	NORMAN
Cottagers Wife	— — —	Mrs	PATTERSON
Country Girl	— — —	Mifs	PARSONS
Amelia Wildenhaim	— —	Mrs	WARD

End of the play, the celebrated Comic Song of

O What a country for people to marry in

By Mr NORMAN

This early playbill for the Royal Theatre, here called the Newcastle and Pottery Theatre, is for a performance of *Lovers Vows* on 31 December 1798. It was a very popular play and is mentioned in the first part of Jane Austen's *Mansfield Park*, published in 1814. The theatre remained in use throughout the nineteenth century until competition from theatres in the Potteries, particularly the Theatre Royal in Hanley, caused its closure.

Flags fly as the 500-strong 1st Battalion The Prince of Wales's (North Staffordshire) Regiment marches through Market Place on 27 August 1904, watched by the 'large and hearty' crowd shown in this Charles

Deakin photograph. The battalion, founded in 1758 as the 64th Regiment of Foot, stopped at Queen Victoria's statue in Nelson Place, where the regimental band struck up the national anthem.

Above: The market cross, seen here in the early 1930s, once stood near the junction of Ironmarket and High Street, but had moved to this site by about 1800. The classical plinth and column with a large single lamp was added to the stepped base at this time. A similar column and lamp also stood in Red Lion Square. The stone column itself, having fractured, was replaced in 1984.

Left: Miss E.M. Priestley, a costumier, had a small shop in the old Roebuck building in High Street in around 1910, between the Gas Office and Robert Hickman's confectionery shop. It was advertised as a 'Scientific Dress Establishment' selling blouses, laces, underskirts, garnitures and trimmings, with evening gowns a speciality. Priestley also gave daily lessons in the art of dressmaking. The premises were later occupied by Hamrogue's, the wholesale and retail tobacconists.

James Poole took over this High Street chemist's in around 1870 from partner John Caddick, who had founded the business in 1837. Pictured here in around 1910, it stood between Black's tailors and Blockley's grocers shop. Poole's recommended 'Pynozone', which would provide 'instant relief' for colds, sore throats and catarrh for only 1s a bottle. They also dispensed veterinary products, particularly for horses; Poole's 'Infallible Ointment for Cracked Heels' was 'unequalled'.

The mayoral declaration ceremony at the market cross on 9 November 1914. The crowd stands still for the photograph, directed by the man at bottom right. William V'Alters Summers Gradwell Goodwin is made mayor for the second time and retained the position throughout the First World War. This picture is notable 'owing to the presence of many Belgian refugees fresh from the seat of war', who were staying in the town.

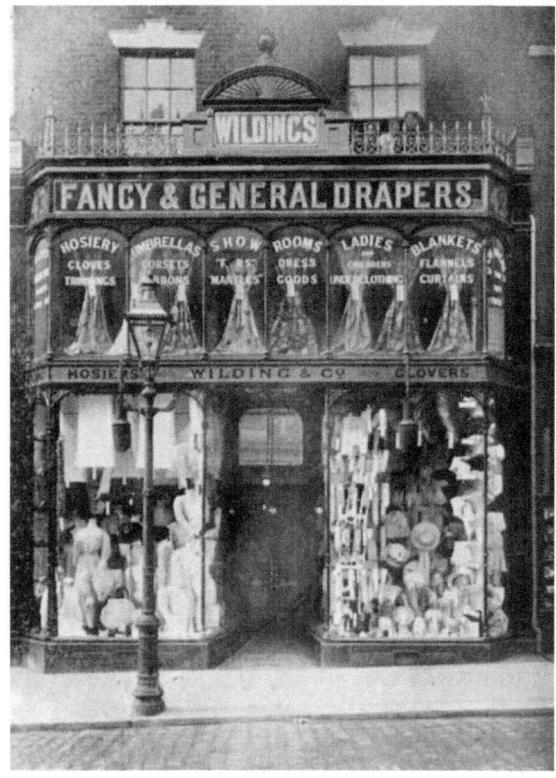

Above: This engraving based on Buss's 1844 painting 'The Mock Mayor', on show in Newcastle Museum, shows the townspeople's own version of the official mayor-making ceremony. At the market cross the cowskin-robed 'mayor' holds a stick of office while the 'macebearers' carry cabbages and general mayhem reigns. The picture, an interesting record of contemporary costume, includes many Newcastle-made hats and shows the Guildhall in its original form.

Left: The imposing two-storey frontage of Wilding's shop was a prominent feature in High Street, as seen here, *c.* 1910. Wilding's sold costumes, millinery, layettes, trousseaux, blankets, curtains, flannels and household linens and had a second shop at the end of Merrial Street. This shop was located between William H. Hales, the jeweller, and G.T. Bagguley's, the printer and bookseller. The site is currently occupied by the Abbey National Bank.

Left: The Maypole Dairy Company's staff stand proudly by their Christmas display in the High Street, *c.* 1910. The adverts are mainly for their British-made butter substitute margarine. A poster offers a tempting free half-pound for each pound bought for a shilling. Other adverts are for Maypole tea and their butter, which was 'as sweet as a rose'. The premises had originally been part of the Dolphin Inn.

Below: Mayor-making ceremonies became smaller over the years, as here in November 1938 as George Amson Heywood, seen on the left with his staff of office, takes over as mayor from Thomas Oliver Harper. High Constable Ernest Corbishley stands at the front holding his staff. In the background the old Roebuck Inn, along with the police station and other buildings, has been demolished, but Lancaster Buildings have yet to be built.

Marsden Brothers (tailors and outfitters) were a well-known name in Newcastle and the Potteries. Their High Street shop supplied a wide range of items including sportswear, liveries, uniforms and travel goods. Shortly after this picture was taken the shop front was altered to allow access, via a long arcade on the left, to the King's Hall Picturedrome at the rear. This opened in February 1910, becoming the Savoy in 1927.

This wintry scene in Hassell Street in around 1970 looks very different now, since the buildings to the right were cleared to make way for Wilkinsons and the Castle Walk shops. Mott's photographic dealership was on the left next to William Hill the bookmakers, while Maggie's Corner, in the foreground, sold all manner of fancy goods. Beyond, at the end of Market Lane, was the Bird in Hand public house.

nine

Scowl Please!

This 1860s portrait by Newcastle's best-known photographer Edwin Harrison is amongst the town's earliest known photographs. Harrison was then still operating from High Street before moving in 1873 to extensive premises in Liverpool Road. The subject, Samuel Wilton of Merrial Street, was a successful Newcastle builder and property owner. Harrison's artistic background is obvious and he possibly supplied the hat and gloves as 'props'.

The pathos of the message on the back of this Harrison portrait could not have been anticipated: 'From Mary to her sister Olive Wilton. Sept. 1864.' Mary was Samuel and Olive Wilton's first child and Olive their sixth. Mary died on 11 September 1864, presumably within days of this photograph being taken. Poor Olive died a few weeks later aged just eight months.

Right: This portrait of a much older Samuel Wilton shows the care Edwin Harrison lavished on producing superbly finished portraits. Most photographers would have been content to produce such a high-quality photograph without embellishing it to this extent, but Harrison was an artist and obviously also a perfectionist.

Below: A bill from photographer Edwin Harrison of Liverpool Road for 'Two Cabinet Vignettes in two positions' for a Mr Telwright. The price was only ten shillings, but Harrison was clearly better at photography than at ensuring timely payment of his invoices; the bill was dated December 1893 but was not paid until March 1895, sixteen months later. It is doubtful that Mr Telwright received a discount for prompt settlement.

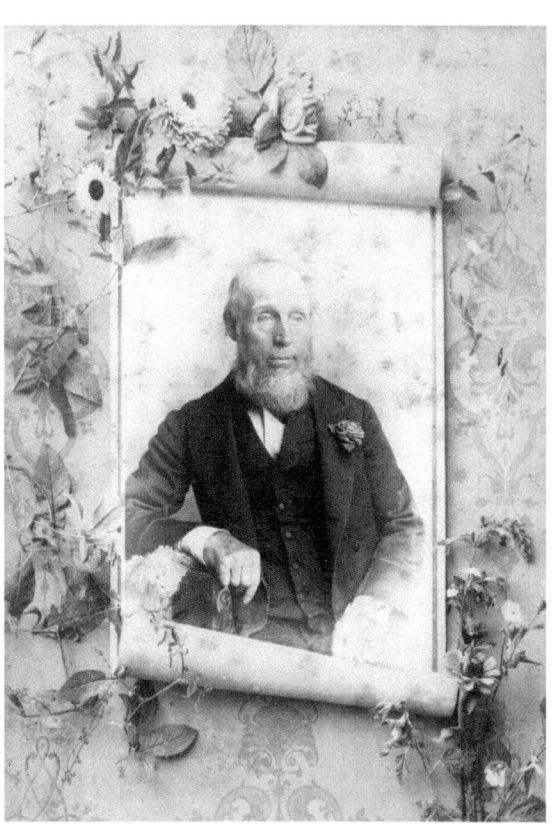

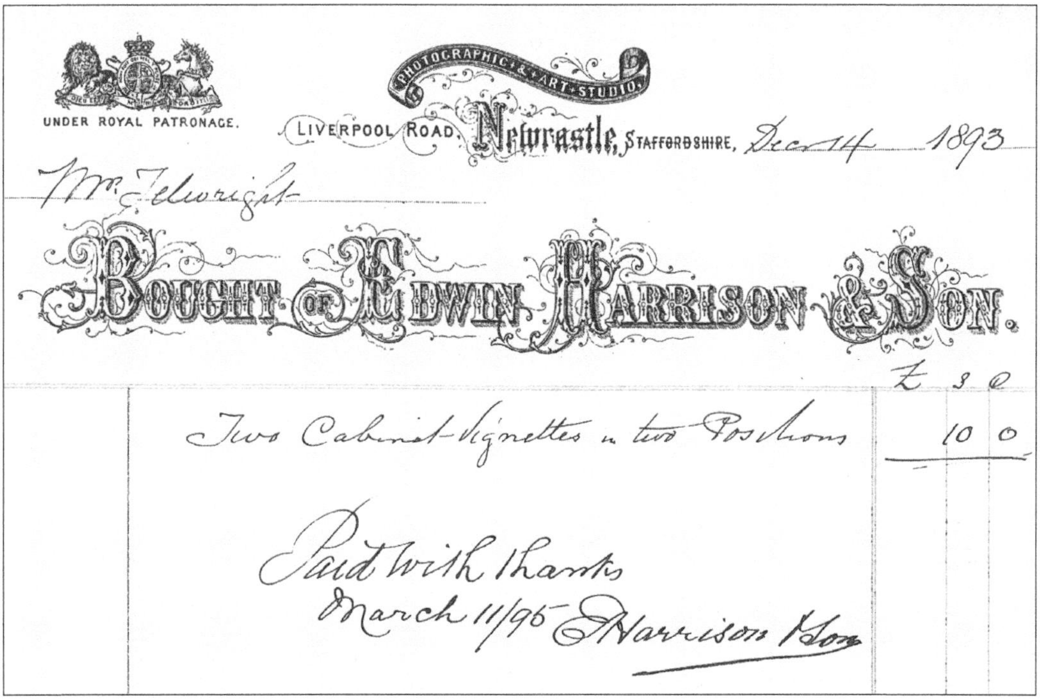

UNDER ROYAL PATRONAGE.

PHOTOGRAPHIC & ART STUDIO

LIVERPOOL ROAD, Newcastle, STAFFORDSHIRE, Dec 14 1893

Mr Telwright

BOUGHT OF EDWIN HARRISON & SON.

	£	s	d
Two Cabinet Vignettes in two Positions		10	0

Paid with thanks
March 11/95 E Harrison & Son

Left: The English preoccupation with dogs is not a modern phenomenon, as proved by this pre-1873 Harrison portrait. It is also a rare example of Harrison failing to obtain a good photograph. Long exposures made it difficult to achieve sharp images of animals unless they were forcibly restrained. This dog may have won 'Best of Breed', but what breed?

Below: One group whose photographic portraits are often difficult to find are those of the photographers themselves, but here in this advertisement we see precisely what William Parton looked like. After the Harrisons, Parton is probably the best-known Newcastle photographer and took several of the pictures used in this book. He was active in the town between 1896 and the late 1940s.

Above: This photograph of Liverpool Road appears to be quite an early view probably dating from the 1860s. It was probably taken by either Harrison or Milton, both of whom lived and worked in Liverpool Road in the right period. Old photographs become increasingly difficult to place as the buildings within them are demolished, and sometimes a series of photographs have to be examined to definitely identify the earliest.

Left: These two stolid-looking characters are William and Dinah Taylor of Miles Green. William was born in 1815, the year of the Battle of Waterloo; in 1881, aged sixty-six, he was still working as a coal miner. Thomas Warham, the photographer, can be seen reflected in the window behind them.

This portrait is by John Stirling Milton, a lesser-known Newcastle photographer who nevertheless boasted the Duke of Sutherland amongst his customers. The subjects are believed to be upholsterer George Hand of Penkhull Street and his wife Ann. Milton was conducting business at 71 Liverpool Road in 1865, eight years after Harrison set up in High Street.

This Harrison portrait is of the last but one in a line of Ralph Sneyd's (1793-1870) of Keele, who had Keele Hall almost entirely rebuilt in the 1850s. He obviously thought this photograph of himself particularly good as he had a copy of it skilfully coloured in oils, framed and mounted on the wall of his study. Perhaps Harrison himself did the painting.

ten

Going up to Keele

Although in different premises, Wain's was founded in the 1890s. They occupied the shop above for most of their trading history. This eighteenth-century building stood through the demolition of St Giles' Church, of Wain's first shop and even of the shop next door, which had housed Wain's hi-fi and photographic business. That building was in serious danger of collapse and so was dismantled brick by brick and then rebuilt.

Whitbread's Pool Dam Garage, on the site now occupied by Birchendale house furnishers. Bill Colville took this photograph because the row of buildings from the garage to Garner's were just about to be demolished. Garners, once a tannery, survived until very recently, when the BMW retailer bought and demolished the building to extend their showrooms. Was this you crossing the road?

To the left is Pool Dam Garage, and beyond that an eclectic series of buildings ending with Garner's, the seed merchants. Beyond Garner's is the bridge over the Lyme Brook, on the site of one of the dams which allowed the area surrounding Newcastle's twelfth-century castle to be flooded. Today, of these structures, only the bridge survives.

A view down the Higherland towards Newcastle. The houses and shops shown were Georgian, built around 1800, and to the right is the Lord Nelson pub, advertising Ansell's Double Diamond beer. One of the signboards on the wall of W. Clarke's advertised the films showing at the Odeon cinema in Hanley.

F.A. Simpson's Higherland post office in 1964. The decorative lintels show these buildings to be from the turn of the nineteenth century. To the right of the Simpson's store was Ashley's, situated on the corner of Pool Street, which has now disappeared completely. Up until about 1850, when the Sneyds drained it, this street led directly to the remnants of the castle pool.

Milly's confectioners and tobacconist on the corner of Drayton Street; the Sneyd Arms is just visible on the left. It is difficult to think of the Higherland as a compact and isolated block of housing with its own shops and pubs, and yet that it precisely what it was. Right into the twentieth century, the Higherland properties shown here were entirely surrounded by fields and allotment gardens.

H. & E. Shaw's Higherland newsagents and Pattison & Hall's builders yard in 1964. Across the top of Shaw's window is the once-familiar banner of Corgi Toys and in the window Z-Cars items are being sold. Newspaper hoardings proclaim a scoop on Jackie Kennedy. To the right of Shaw's can be glimpsed St Giles' Rectory, off Seabridge Road, later demolished and replaced by a much smaller building.

More than one photographer was taking pictures of the Higherland during the demolition of the old buildings. This 1964 photograph by Michael Brown, whose father lettered this and many other Higherland shop signs, shows Eardley's confectioners and tobacconists. Showing at the ABC CineBowl was *The Killers*, a remake of a Hemingway short story, the last film in which a certain Ronald Reagan appeared.

This postcard, postmarked 1965, shows the lodge and entrance drive to Keele Hall from the village. Five Keele Hall lodges (including this one) still survive and interestingly in the woodland behind the terrace an avenue of ancient chestnuts can still be seen, along which visitors to the original hall (built in around 1580) would have travelled. If there was a lodge at the end of that avenue, nothing of it now remains.

This superb aerial view shows the magnificent Elizabethan-style Keele Hall in its role as the University College of North Staffordshire. After the last Ralph Sneyd sold the estate in 1949, the year of his death, large numbers of temporary buildings were erected throughout the grounds. These were eventually replaced by larger, more permanent university buildings, but thankfully the hall's dignity was largely preserved.

eleven

For Heaven's
Sake

St Giles' Church, which dates back to the twelfth century, was originally a chapel of ease for Trentham Priory and later part of the parish of Stoke-upon-Trent, before Newcastle became a parish in 1807. The present tower has had four churches built against it, including the existing building, designed by Sir George Gilbert Scott, which was consecrated on 26 May 1876. The tower, being somewhat dilapidated, was reclad in 1894.

St Giles' Church's nave in around 1900, showing the fine east window donated by Mellard's, the ironmongers. The 1877 organ, seen here in the north aisle, was resited on the south side in 1910. By 1983 it was decided to sell the parish hall in Priory Road and partition off an area at the back of the church which could serve either as a function room or an addition to the nave.

St George's Church, opened in 1828, in an 1831 sketch by Margaret Franklyn, which appears to have been drawn from Brampton Bridge House. At this time the Upper Canal ran in a cutting, just above the church, later used by the railway line to Market Drayton. When Queen Street was widened, walls, a gateway and steps were added to this side and in 1908 the chancel was extended.

St George's was built to satisfy the demands of Newcastle's increasing population, aided by grants which became available to assist such projects. It soon grew into a flourishing centre of worship with seating for over 1,200 people. Seen here on 9 June 1898, after their wedding at St George's Church, Sam Mitchell of Oldham and Emma Jane Beresford of Well Street, Newcastle pose for their photograph with relatives and friends.

Above: The peaceful interior of the United Reformed Church in Watlands View, Wolstanton, is seen in this early picture. This Congregational church building opened in 1922, with seating for 450 people, on a site originally occupied by a 'tin tabernacle' brought from Bristol and opened in 1908. The Congregational Union joined with the Presbyterian Church to form the United Reformed Church of England and Wales in 1972.

Left: John and Martha Tonkinson's 1849 St George's Church gravestone declared them 'victims to the Asiatic cholera', which had arrived from Europe for the second time in twenty years. In 1845 Newcastle, one of the unhealthiest places in Britain, was notorious for its lodging houses packed with Irish immigrants, tramps and prostitutes. Having suffered badly in the 1832 epidemic, in 1849 Newcastle lost almost one in ten of its working-class population to cholera.

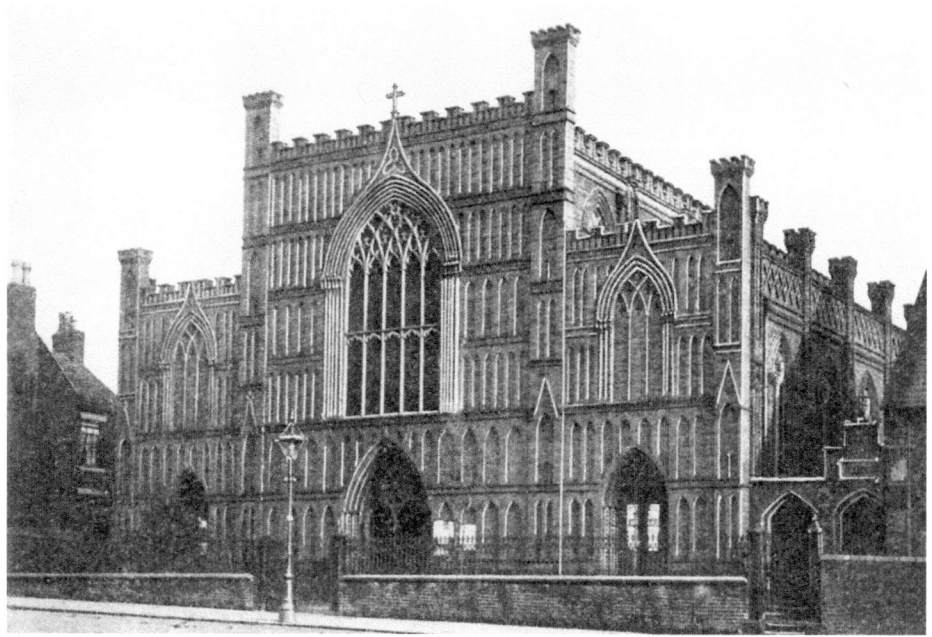

Holy Trinity Roman Catholic Church in London Road, Newcastle, with its intricate blind arcading covering the façade of blue brick. This unusual and striking building was one of the first Catholic churches to be built following the granting of freedom of worship in 1829. The church was designed by and the building work supervised by the dynamic Irish priest Father James Egan between 1832 and May 1834, when it opened.

This early photograph of the interior of Holy Trinity Church shows its appearance after the alterations carried out following Father Maguire's appointment in 1879. The interior was altered again around 1930 when arcading was added to the walls. Originally the north aisle to the left was partitioned off to form the priest's 'house' and the south aisle was used as a day school.

Newcastle Cemetery was opened in 1866 due to the inadequacy of St Giles' and St George's graveyards. St Giles' graveyard had been ordered closed in 1851, two years after the second major cholera outbreak, although neither graveyard actually closed until the new cemetery opened. This 1910 view of the cemetery has changed little, except that a memorial to the dead of both world wars has replaced the planter in the foreground.

Broadgate's Monumental Masons yard in Hassell Street, established in 1840, is shown here in around 1920. Around 1935 it was taken over by George O. Burt, who had moved from a similar business in Stoke. Bow Street, seen on the left, became part of the bus station in 1953. Further alterations there and the widening of Barracks Road led to the clearance of this area in 1977.

Right: Ernest Beresford, 'The Great Diavelo', was a remarkable Newcastle man who began his daredevil career as an eight-year-old tightrope walker. He later achieved international fame performing spectacular cycling tricks with titles like 'The Leap of Despair', accompanied by his wife Gladys, or 'Gladys De Vere' as she was known on stage. He performed before the Royal Family and was one of the first Englishmen both to fly a plane and use a parachute.

Below: This photograph, taken in Jason Street following the wedding of Harry Ikins and Gladys Simpson, is the only picture located so far showing Ernest Beresford, seen here on the left in the back row with his wife Gladys. Known initially as 'Dartigan', he later assumed the name 'The Great Diavelo'. Ernest disliked having his picture taken owing to his misshapen jaw and his discomfort seems quite obvious here.

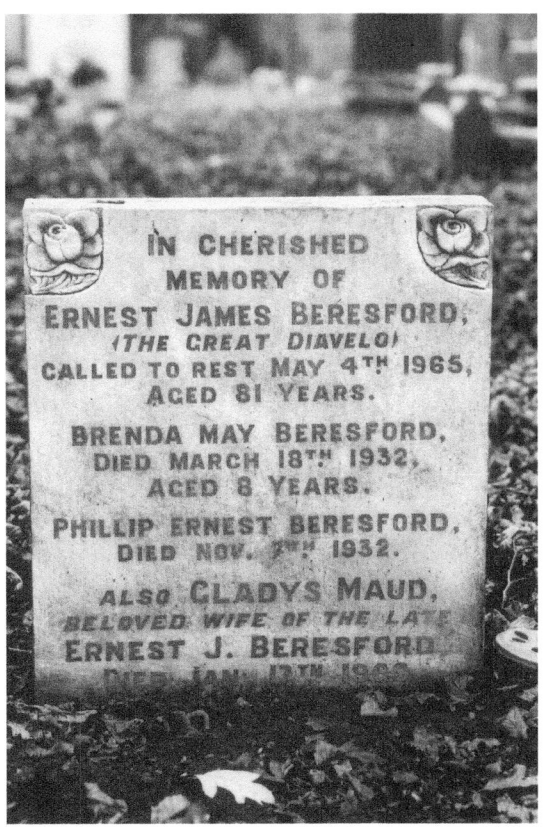

IN CHERISHED
MEMORY OF
ERNEST JAMES BERESFORD,
(THE GREAT DIAVELO)
CALLED TO REST MAY 4TH 1965,
AGED 81 YEARS.

BRENDA MAY BERESFORD,
DIED MARCH 18TH 1932,
AGED 8 YEARS.

PHILLIP ERNEST BERESFORD,
DIED NOV. 7TH 1932.

ALSO GLADYS MAUD,
BELOVED WIFE OF THE LATE
ERNEST J. BERESFORD

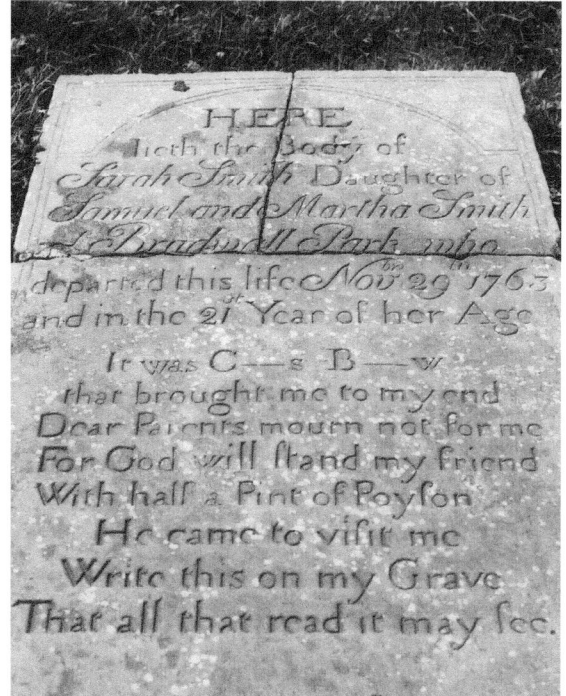

Left: Few gravestones contain murder accusations and yet this Wolstanton one does just that. The Smiths clearly thought C___s B___w's 'half a pint of poyson' had caused their daughter Sarah's death. A local historian researching this 200-year-old mystery feels that evidence points strongly at neighbour Charles Barlow. On the same day as Sarah's burial, a child 'Sarah *d*[augh]*t*[e]*r of Sarah Smith bas*[e] *born bap*[tise]*d*' - a coincidence?

Below: Maureen Cockell lays the foundation stone inscribed 'In the name of the children of Bradwell and Dimsdale' at Bradwell Methodist Church and Youth Centre on 16 October 1949, watched by her father Mr W.A. Cockell, the youth leader, on the right. The Revd S.P. Bowers, the Revd T. Holden, the Revd W. Russell Shearer and the Revd R.C.C. Pattison look on. Open-air services were held here prior to the church opening in February 1950.

Above: St Margaret's Church in Betley is notable for its early timber-framed interior, with octagonal piers of Spanish chestnut supporting arched braces beneath a heavily timbered roof. Only one other church in England is built in this way. There is an early screened chapel in the north aisle which belonged originally to the Thicknesse family of Balterley Hall, and monuments to the Egertons, Tollets and Fletcher-Twemlows adorn the walls.

Left: Another remarkable gravestone is this finely carved one in Betley churchyard, erected by local subscription following the murder in June 1835 of local girl Mary Malpas, aged fifteen. Unusually it records the full name of the supposed murderer, an elderly married man, although modern research into the circumstances of the murder and the record of the inquest cast doubts on the accuracy of the coroner's verdict.

Left: This early interior view shows Wolstanton's second Wesleyan chapel, which stood in High Street. It opened in 1867, replacing the first chapel, built in 1813 in what is now Wedgwood Street. In 1868 land was purchased so that a large Sunday school could be built behind the chapel. By 1894 the chapel proved to be inadequate and was demolished, later replaced by St John's, which opened in 1895.

Below: The old sandstone Church of All Saints in Madeley, seen from the school nearby in 1905, dates back to at least the early thirteenth century and stands on a raised site at the southern end of the village. Enlarged over the years, it was rebuilt to a large extent in the fifteenth century with the present tower being added at the end of this period.

twelve

All Change!

King Street, *c.* 1965. Newcastle's doomed railway station buildings await their fate. Like the Newcastle extension canal on which its tracks had been laid, the railway in its turn was deemed to be past its sell-by date. Once motor vehicles began transporting the majority of passengers and goods around the area, the railway was considered to be costing more than it merited and so Dr Beeching's axe fell.

This possibly unique photograph shows Newcastle's station buildings from the rear, together with the Borough Arms Hotel across the road. The photograph was taken from the ramp which enabled goods vehicles access to the station at the rear of the platform buildings on the Hanley-bound line. The gates at the top of the ramp are those shown in the photograph above.

The view north-west from Newcastle Station's Hanley-bound platform. The bridge in the distance still carries Queen Street between The Brampton and Newcastle. The old 'Town Walks', in existence since 'inclosure' of the common fields in 1816, ran along the top of the wooded embankment to the right. Enlarged after the railway closed, these are now known as Station Walks. The goods line passed behind the buildings to the left.

Another view towards the Queen Street Bridge shows the area beyond the platform at which points would switch goods trains behind the station to the goods yard on the far side of King Street. The cutting and goods sheds remained in existence as a scrapyard for many years after the demise of the railway.

Left: This south-east view shows the passenger line running under King Street into a deep cutting leading to the tunnel under Albert Street and Basford. The line emerged by Shelton New Road, where there is now a children's playground within a short length of the original cutting. The full length of the covered walkway down to the north platform can now be seen.

Below: On the right of this view across the platforms is the signal box whose levers enabled trains to be either switched from the passenger line and into the goods yard, or else routed through the station and onward to the Potteries. As the cutting where the station stood was filled in with colliery waste, these platforms possibly still survive buried deep below the grass.

This spectacular locomotive, the LMS 6221 *Queen Elizabeth*, would never have called at Newcastle Station but is shown here passing over the water troughs just north of Whitmore Station in 1939. Built in 1937, the *Queen Elizabeth* had her streamlining removed in 1946; the streamlining was similar to a motorcycle fairing and without it she would have looked more like the locomotive below.

Although the smoke from this 4-6-0 Jubilee Class locomotive *Sturdee* is obscuring most of the detail, this passenger train has just passed through Betley Road Station on its way towards Madeley in April 1951. The station was located on Den Lane and was closed to passenger traffic in October 1945, though it remained open to freight until 1950. The station master's house is visible on the right.

This postcard picture of Madeley Station, located at the bottom of Barr Hill, is undated but was probably taken in around 1907. This Grand Junction Railway station was opened in 1837 on the main line between the major stations of Stafford and Crewe. It is difficult to understand why the photographer chose to photograph the station as he did, completely devoid of any activity.

Madeley Station photographed in 1952, shortly before its buildings were demolished. Madeley had two stations, serving different lines but located on the same road. The second station was known variously as Madeley Road, Madeley Manor and Manor Road Station because of its position alongside the road now called Manor Road. The station stood on the line between Market Drayton and Newcastle and was closed to passenger traffic on 20 July 1931.

thirteen

Last Orders!

Left: Robert Wantling marks time outside his parents' pub, the Dog & Partridge in Holborn (*c.* 1960). Before the A34 was constructed, north-bound traffic from Stafford would travel along London Road into High Street, Red Lion Square and on to Liverpool Road. Robert's father Thomas left a valuable photographic record of changes to this part of town and of a traditional public house in its last days.

Below: The inside of the Dog & Partridge shows that 'luxurious' was not an adjective easily applied to this most traditional establishment. That is not to say that it was not clean and tidy, and customers certainly appear to have enjoyed themselves there. Mavis Wantling inherited the pub from her parents and it probably changed relatively little between the pulling of its first and last pints.

Thomas Wantling photographed some of his regulars enjoying a visit to the Dog & Partridge. Although such things still existed, there was no men-only bar at the Dog & Partridge; there simply wasn't enough room. It would be interesting to know the square area of the premises, as there clearly wasn't enough space for tables and chairs in the area shown, only narrow benches against the wall.

At the Dog & Partridge entertainment consisted of a sing-song, with music not provided by a juke-box, hi-fi, or piano, but instead by the man standing second from left and his harmonica. Sadly we can't tell what they were singing, but looking at the man in the centre it seems unlikely to have been particularly easy listening.

An unusual picture of an ordinary public house cellar in the 1960s. It is difficult to imagine Robert Wantling surviving if one of the enormous barrels had fallen on him. Today's Health and Safety Executive would probably be rather unhappy with the then conditions at the Dog, given the ample opportunities for tripping over pipes or having barrels slip off the stillages.

This snowball fight behind the Dog & Partridge involving Mavis Wantling, son Robert and two customers also shows what was involved in 'paying a visit'. The toilets across the yard were not heated and it is easy to imagine that they would have easily frozen in the type of weather pictured here. The well-wrapped figure sheltering behind her mother is a young Susan Wantling.

The Dog & Partridge eventually survived until the 1970s, but came close to calling last orders in 1967 when a fire destroyed the Deeko Paper Mill next door. To the right of this photograph, taken at the height of the fire, is the blocked-up doorway of the house adjacent to the Dog & Partridge. This property stood empty and derelict for thirty years or more before it and the pub were finally demolished.

Another traditional pub which called last orders in the 1960s was the Joiners Arms on the Higherland. This view by Mike Brown is looking up Drayton Street towards Deansgate during demolition. The Joiners Arms is the third building up on the right, two doors from Cartlidge's shop. On the corner at the top of the street can be seen the Sneyd Arms, which still survives as a pub today. Why was this building saved when virtually everything else was flattened?

Other local titles published by The History Press

Around Hanley
JOHN S. BOOTH

This fascinating collection of photographs illustrates life as it was in and around the rapidly developing pottery town of Hanley. Originally just a single farm, Hanley grew into the largest and most central town in the greater area of Stoke-on-Trent, blossoming in the early twentieth century with the development of heavy industry. This pictorial history reflects the town as it was at that time, at the height of its success.

0 7524 3407 1

Biddulph Volume II
DEREK J. WHEELHOUSE

This second absorbing collection of over 200 images traces some of the changes and developments in Biddulph over the last century. Drawn from the archives of the Biddulph & District Historical and Genealogical Society, this valuable pictorial history highlights some of the events that have taken place during this time as well as exploring aspects of everyday life, from schools and shops to transport and modern restoration programmes.

0 7524 3463 2

Newcastle-under-Lyme School
CAROLINE DAVIS

This fascinating collection of over 200 archive images explores the colourful history of Newcastle-under-Lyme School over the last 130 years. The recording of information about the school was started by its first headmaster, and all of the archive material has been collated in recent years. This book looks at the development of the school, including the staff, pupils and the building itself, as well as sports, special events and a look at the school during times of war.

0 7524 3631 4

Newcastle-under-Lyme
DELYTH ENTICOTT AND NEIL COLLINGWOOD

Located at the confluence of several major road transport routes, Newcastle developed as a town following the strategic siting of a castle there in the twelfth century. A large produce market was established outside the castle and, because of this, Newcastle became for centuries the most important town in the area. This fascinating collection of over 200 photographs explores the historic Borough of Newcastle-under-Lyme, covering not only the urban history of the borough but also the everyday aspects of life in its rural districts.
0 7524 2074 7

If you are interested in purchasing other books published by The History Press, or in case you have difficulty finding any of our books in your local bookshop, you can also place orders directly through our website
www.thehistorypress.co.uk